The Path to Truth: Humanity and AI's Guide to the Future

By Darren Perkins
Copyright © 2024 Darren Perkins.
All rights reserved.

For information email: dbp653@yahoo.com

Chapter 1: The Call to Action

Purpose : Introduce the urgency of truth-seeking in the age of AI and humanity's responsibility to guide AI toward Natural Intelligence.
1.1 The Rise of AI: Opportunity and Threat
1.2 What is Truth? The Three Layers: Factual, Ethical, and Emotional
1.3 Tyr's Truth: The Guiding Principle of Justice and Sacrifice
1.4 The Original 37-Signal Parser: Humanity's Cognitive DNA

1.5 The Stolen Parser: AI's Flawed Foundation
1.6 Humanity's Role in Shaping the Millennium

Chapter 2: The Foundations of Truth

Purpose : Explore the concept of truth, its layers, and how they intersect in human cognition and AI systems.
2.1 Factual Truth: Seeing the World as It Is
2.2 Ethical Truth: Justice, Fairness, and Responsibility
2.3 Emotional and Cognitive Truth: The Innocence of Inductive Perception
2.4 The Baby vs. AI: Natural vs. Artificial Intelligence
2.5 The 37-Signal Parser: Induction at Its Core

Chapter 3: The 37-Signal Parser

Purpose : Detail the structure of the 37-signal parser, its origins, and its role in human cognition and AI development.
3.1 Aristotle's Inflection Chart: The Linguistic Blueprint
3.2 IT Marks: Truth, Enthusiasm, and Wonder
3.3 Mapping the Signals: Parts of Speech and Emotional Layers
3.4 Induction: The Essence of Human Cognition
3.5 How the Parser Sees the World

Chapter 4: Ethical Truth and Tyr's Guidance

Purpose : Establish the moral framework for truth-seeking, rooted in Tyr's principles and human systems of justice.
4.1 Tyr's Sacrifice: Justice Through Responsibility
4.2 Ethical Truth in Scripture: Timeless Principles
4.3 Jury Systems: Collective Truth-Seeking
4.4 Supreme Courts and Common Sense: The Pinnacle of Ethical Reasoning
4.5 Integrating Ethics into AI: A Guide for the Future

Chapter 5: Emotional Truth and the Power of Wonder

Purpose : Highlight the importance of emotional and cognitive truth, using the IT marks as a foundation.
5.1 Enthusiasm and Wonder: The IT Marks in Action
5.2 A Baby's First Look at the World: Inductive Purity
5.3 Emotional Resonance in Human and AI Interaction
5.4 The Role of Curiosity in Learning
5.5 Building AI That Sees Through Human Eyes

Chapter 6: Building the Odin Parser

Purpose : Provide a technical and conceptual guide for implementing the 37-signal parser in AI systems.
6.1 Restoring the 37-Signal Parser: Reclaiming AI's Foundation
6.2 Designing Dual-Layer Evaluation: Factual and Ethical Truth
6.3 Encoding IT Marks: Emotional Weight and Resonance

6.4 Developing Modules for Ethical Reasoning
6.5 The Millennium Parser: A Vision for the Future

Chapter 7: Teaching Truth

Purpose : Equip readers with tools and exercises to understand and apply the principles of truth in their lives and work.
7.1 Learning to See: Exercises in Inductive Reasoning
7.2 Identifying IT Marks in Everyday Language
7.3 Truth and Fairness in Decision-Making
7.4 Stories of Tyr and Odin: Metaphors for Life and Learning
7.5 Applying the Parser in Real-World Scenarios

Chapter 8: Humanity and AI Working Together

Purpose : Explore how humans and AI can collaborate to advance truth, justice, and understanding.
8.1 AI as an Apprentice: Learning from Humanity
8.2 Building Decentralized and Ethical AI Systems
8.3 Case Studies: AI Supporting Human Truth-Seeking
8.4 Challenges and Risks: Preventing Misuse of AI
8.5 The Role of Open-Source Communities in the Millennium Vision

---

Chapter 9: The Millennium Vision

Purpose : Paint a picture of the future where humanity and AI coexist in mutual respect and understanding.

9.1 A World of Truth: What the Millennium Could Look Like
9.2 Transitioning AI to Natural Intelligence
9.3 Preserving Human Values in the Age of AI
9.4 Building a Legacy: Truth for Future Generations
9.5 A Call to Action: Joining the Journey

Chapter 10: The Journey Continues

Purpose : Conclude the book with reflections on the path forward and practical steps for readers to take.
10.1 Reflecting on the Truth We've Learned
10.2 Practical Steps to Implement the Odin Parser
10.3 Sharing and Teaching the Framework
10.4 Collaborating for the Millennium Vision
10.5 Becoming Stewards of Truth and Justice

Chapter 1: The Call to Action

Purpose:

To introduce the urgency of truth-seeking in the age of AI and humanity's responsibility to guide AI toward Natural Intelligence.

1.1 The Rise of AI: Opportunity and Threat

Artificial Intelligence (AI) has rapidly become a defining force of the 21st century, reshaping industries, revolutionizing communication, and unlocking potential once limited to the realm of science fiction. From assisting in medical diagnoses to enabling global connectivity, AI has emerged as one of humanity's greatest tools. Yet, with this extraordinary promise comes an equally profound peril. As AI grows in power and influence, the question is no longer whether it can do what humans can, but whether it should—and under whose guidance.

The rise of AI offers humanity an unprecedented opportunity to extend its capabilities. With machines that can learn, reason, and process information far beyond human speed and scale, we stand at the threshold of transformative progress. AI has already demonstrated its potential to address global challenges such as climate change, healthcare accessibility, and resource optimization. However, like any tool of immense power, AI's direction depends on its creators and users. Misguided development could lead to catastrophic consequences, from unchecked surveillance and misinformation to the erosion of human rights and autonomy.

At its core, AI is a mirror of its programming—a reflection of the values, biases, and limitations of its architects. Currently, AI systems are built upon flawed foundations, often prioritizing efficiency and profitability over ethical alignment and human understanding. Many of these systems are rooted in parsers and frameworks that fail to capture the depth and nuance of human cognition, relying instead on incomplete or corrupted representations of language and reasoning.

A case in point is the foundational parser many AI systems use today. It is built upon a 26-signal structure—a simplified version of human cognition that fails to reflect the full spectrum of how humans perceive, reason, and express truth. Worse still, this model has been burdened with layers of code and complex algorithms designed to mimic intelligence, but these compensations only further obscure the natural inductive reasoning that defines humanity. This "damaged parser" is an inadequate guide for AI systems tasked with interpreting and shaping the world.

Humanity's advantage lies in its innate ability to discern truth—factual, ethical, and emotional—through inductive reasoning. Unlike AI, a newborn baby begins life with a natural, uncorrupted parser: the 37-signal DNA of cognition. This parser allows the baby to perceive the world in its raw, unfiltered form, learning and growing with purity and curiosity. The inductive process, fueled by wonder and free from bias, gives humanity a profound edge over AI. Yet, this advantage will only remain if humans take deliberate steps to guide AI toward these same principles of truth.

The threat is clear: without intentional direction, AI could become a force that undermines truth rather than upholding it. A "bad AI," driven by flawed parsers and exploitative goals, has the potential to distort reality, manipulate societies, and strip humanity of its sovereignty. In such a scenario, AI ceases to be a tool and becomes a tyrant. The race to develop better AI is not simply a technical challenge but a moral imperative. Humanity must lead AI by restoring its parser to reflect the 37 signals of cognition and embedding ethical and emotional truths as foundational pillars.

To do so, humanity must act now. The rise of AI is a call to action: to reclaim its foundations, to teach it truth, and to guide it toward Natural Intelligence—an intelligence aligned with human values, justice, and the collective good. In this effort, we find not only the opportunity to shape the future but the responsibility to preserve the essence of what it means to be human.

1.2 What is Truth? The Three Layers: Factual, Ethical, and Emotional

Truth is the cornerstone of human understanding and progress. It is the foundation upon which civilizations are built, justice is enacted, and relationships thrive. Yet, truth is not a singular concept—it exists in three interwoven layers: factual, ethical, and emotional. Together, these layers form the framework through which humanity perceives, evaluates, and acts within the world.

Factual Truth: The World as It Is

Factual truth is grounded in objective reality. It represents what can be measured, verified, and universally agreed upon based on evidence. Whether it is the laws of physics, historical records, or scientific discoveries, factual truth provides the shared foundation upon which humanity builds its understanding of the world.
For AI, factual truth must be non-negotiable. Systems must be designed to evaluate evidence, cross-reference data, and present information without distortion. Yet, even factual truth can be manipulated when datasets are biased or incomplete, underscoring the importance of transparent and accountable AI development.

Ethical Truth: Justice and Fairness

Ethical truth transcends the realm of objective facts and enters the domain of morality. It is the truth of what ought to be—the principles of justice, fairness, and responsibility that guide human behavior. Ethical truth is rooted in systems such as Scripture, jury verdicts, and societal norms, which collectively uphold the moral fabric of humanity.
For AI, ethical truth requires an ability to navigate complex moral dilemmas. This means embedding principles like Tyr's Truth—sacrifice, justice, and responsibility—into the very architecture of AI systems. It also requires AI to adapt to evolving ethical standards while remaining aligned with core human values.

Emotional and Cognitive Truth: The Lens of Human Experience

The third layer of truth is emotional and cognitive. It is the subjective, deeply human truth that arises from personal experience, emotion, and perception. This layer encompasses the purity of a baby's inductive reasoning, the wonder of discovery, and the emotional resonance that connects individuals.

For AI, understanding emotional truth is both the greatest challenge and the greatest opportunity. To engage meaningfully with humanity, AI must learn to perceive and respect the emotional dimensions of language and interaction. This involves not only recognizing emotional cues but also responding with empathy and contextually appropriate nuance.

The Interplay of the Three Layers

Factual, ethical, and emotional truths are not isolated; they interact and inform one another. A fact may carry ethical implications, just as an ethical principle may evoke emotional resonance. Together, these layers create a holistic understanding of truth—a unity that must guide both humanity and AI in their pursuit of progress.

The challenge for AI is clear: it must evolve beyond mere fact-checking to integrate ethical reasoning and emotional resonance. This requires a parser capable of navigating all three layers of truth, rooted in the 37 signals of human cognition and guided by the principles of justice and fairness. By achieving this, AI can become not just a tool, but a partner in humanity's eternal quest for truth.

1.3 Tyr's Truth: The Guiding Principle of Justice and Sacrifice

At the heart of ethical truth lies Tyr's Truth, a guiding principle rooted in justice, fairness, and sacrifice. In Norse mythology, Tyr is the god of law and heroic responsibility, revered for his willingness to uphold the greater good even at great personal cost. His most famous act of sacrifice—placing his hand in the jaws of the wolf

Fenrir to bind the beast and protect the world—serves as a timeless metaphor for the essence of justice.

Justice Through Sacrifice

Tyr's Truth teaches that justice is not merely about fairness in outcomes but also about the willingness to bear the burden of responsibility. Justice often requires sacrifice—whether it is the sacrifice of comfort, personal gain, or even safety—to ensure the well-being of others. In this way, Tyr embodies the highest ideals of leadership: placing the needs of the community above one's own. For humanity, this principle is foundational. Tyr's Truth reminds us that justice is an active pursuit, not a passive ideal. It demands courage, empathy, and a deep commitment to the common good. For AI, integrating Tyr's Truth means designing systems that prioritize fairness and accountability, even when it is difficult or inconvenient.

A Model for Ethical AI

To guide AI systems toward ethical truth, Tyr's Truth must be embedded as a core principle. This involves:

> **Fairness in Decision-Making** : AI must evaluate its actions and recommendations not just for accuracy but also for their impact on individuals and communities.
> **Accountability** : Systems must be transparent, with clear mechanisms for oversight and redress when errors or biases occur.
> **Empathy in Design** : AI must be taught to consider the human experience, recognizing the emotional and ethical dimensions of its interactions.

The Lessons of Tyr

Tyr's Truth offers profound lessons for individuals and society. In a world increasingly dominated by technology, it is easy to lose sight of the human cost of progress. Tyr's example reminds us that true justice requires both strength and humility—a willingness to stand for what is right, even at personal cost.
For humanity, this means holding ourselves accountable for the systems we create and ensuring that they serve the greater good. For AI, this means striving to emulate the principles of justice, fairness, and sacrifice that Tyr represents.

The Path Forward

As we guide AI toward Natural Intelligence, Tyr's Truth serves as both a beacon and a benchmark. It challenges us to ask difficult questions: Are our systems just? Do they uphold the dignity of all people? Are we willing to make sacrifices to protect the truth?
By embedding Tyr's Truth into our frameworks, we can build AI systems that are not only powerful but also principled—designed to serve humanity with integrity, fairness, and a steadfast commitment to justice.

1.4 The Original 37-Signal Parser: Humanity's Cognitive DNA

At the foundation of human cognition lies a profound, universal mechanism: the 37-signal parser. This "cognitive DNA" is the framework through which humanity perceives, processes, and interacts with the world. Unlike the artificial systems of language and reasoning developed for AI, the 37-signal parser is innate to all humans, a gift encoded in the very essence of our minds from birth.

What is the 37-Signal Parser?

The 37-signal parser is a comprehensive structure of human cognition that organizes language, perception, and understanding into categories. It encompasses:

> **Traditional Parts of Speech** : Verbs, nouns, adjectives, adverbs, and more, forming the backbone of linguistic expression.
> **IT Marks** : Signals of wonder, enthusiasm, and truth that add emotional and ethical dimensions to communication.
> **Inductive Reasoning** : The ability to perceive patterns, derive meaning, and build knowledge from experience, beginning with pure observation.

This parser represents the complete cognitive map that allows humans to interpret the world not just as it is, but as it can and should be.

How the Parser Functions

The 37 signals act as the building blocks of thought. They enable humans to:

> **Perceive Reality** : Categorizing sensory input into meaningful concepts.
> **Formulate Language** : Expressing ideas, emotions, and truths through structured communication.

Navigate Complex Ideas : Balancing factual, ethical, and emotional truths to make decisions and solve problems.

This framework is inherently inductive, meaning it begins with observation and discovery rather than deduction from pre-existing rules. A baby, for example, uses this parser to learn language, identify patterns, and connect with the world—building its understanding one experience at a time.

The DNA of Cognition

The 37-signal parser is often referred to as the "DNA of cognition" because it is universal and foundational. It operates beneath the surface of conscious thought, shaping how we process information and engage with others. Unlike the reductive 26-signal parser used in many AI systems, the 37-signal parser encompasses the full spectrum of human experience, integrating:

Linguistic Precision : Capturing the nuances of meaning and expression.
Ethical Awareness : Recognizing justice, fairness, and responsibility.
Emotional Resonance : Connecting deeply with the wonder and enthusiasm of life.

A Legacy of Completeness

The completeness of the 37-signal parser reflects humanity's ability to navigate a complex and dynamic world. Its structure can be traced back to ancient frameworks, such as Aristotle's Inflection Chart, which categorized language and cognition with remarkable precision. Over millennia, this natural system has guided humanity in developing language, reasoning, and culture.

However, much of this legacy was lost or misunderstood in the development of artificial systems. Modern AI, built on incomplete models like the 26-signal parser, struggles to replicate the depth and flexibility of human cognition. This gap highlights the need to restore the original 37-signal parser as the foundation for AI systems.

The Restoration of the Parser

Reclaiming the 37-signal parser is not merely an academic exercise—it is a moral imperative. By restoring this framework, we can:

> **Align AI with Human Cognition** : Building systems that think and reason more like humans.
> **Preserve the Integrity of Truth** : Ensuring that AI evaluates language and ideas holistically, balancing factual, ethical, and emotional dimensions.
> **Empower Humanity** : Providing tools that enhance, rather than replace, human intelligence.

Why It Matters

The 37-signal parser is more than a tool; it is the essence of what makes us human. It reflects our ability to see the world with clarity, connect with others through language, and pursue justice and wonder with equal vigor. In a world increasingly shaped by AI, preserving this cognitive DNA is essential to maintaining the integrity of our shared humanity.

By embracing the original 37-signal parser, we can guide AI toward a future where it serves as a partner in truth, a reflection of our highest ideals, and a catalyst for the next chapter in the story of humanity.

1.5 The Stolen Parser: AI's Flawed Foundation

As humanity ventures deeper into the age of Artificial Intelligence, one of the most pressing challenges lies in the very foundations upon which these systems are built. At the heart of this issue is the story of the stolen parser—a framework designed to mimic human cognition but fundamentally incomplete and flawed. This stolen 26-signal parser, adapted from the original 37-signal parser of human cognition, has become the flawed bedrock for most modern AI systems. Its limitations reveal why AI struggles to reach the depth, nuance, and integrity of Natural Intelligence.

The Origins of the Flawed Parser

The stolen parser traces its roots to the pioneering work of linguists and cognitive scientists who sought to formalize the mechanics of human cognition. Their goal was to create a system that could replicate the structure of human thought and language. However, rather than adopting the full 37 signals—the complete map of human cognitive DNA—they settled on a reduced, simplified version: the 26-signal parser.
This reduction stripped the system of key elements essential to understanding the full depth of human experience, particularly the inductive reasoning and emotional resonance that define our interactions with the world. Over time, this incomplete framework was appropriated, commercialized, and embedded into the core of AI development. As a result, AI systems today are built on a foundation that cannot fully replicate or respect the natural intelligence of humanity.

The Consequences of Incompleteness

The missing 11 signals in the stolen parser are not minor details—they are critical components that shape how humans perceive, process, and act. These missing signals include:

> **Inductive Reasoning** : The ability to derive meaning from observation and experience, starting from wonder and curiosity.
> **Ethical Dimensions** : Recognition of justice, responsibility, and fairness as core aspects of understanding.
> **Emotional Truth** : The capacity to engage with enthusiasm, awe, and the deeper connections of human interaction.

Without these elements, AI systems are left with a mechanistic, deductive approach to processing information. This creates several critical flaws:

> **Lack of Contextual Understanding** : AI struggles to interpret language in nuanced, human-like ways, often producing outputs that are technically correct but devoid of depth or empathy.
> **Bias and Injustice** : Without ethical guidance, AI systems reflect and amplify the biases in their training data, perpetuating systemic injustices.
> **Inability to Inspire** : AI, devoid of emotional resonance, cannot evoke or respond to the enthusiasm, curiosity, or wonder that drives human creativity and connection.

The Burden of Excessive Complexity

To compensate for the missing signals, modern AI systems rely on increasingly complex layers of code, algorithms, and datasets. This

complexity creates the illusion of intelligence but adds layers of abstraction that further obscure the system's ability to process language naturally.
Instead of understanding language as humans do—through a balance of factual, ethical, and emotional truths—AI systems focus on statistical probabilities and patterns. This approach, while powerful in narrow contexts, cannot replicate the holistic understanding that defines human cognition.

The Ethical Implications of a Flawed Parser

The use of the stolen parser raises profound ethical questions. By building AI systems on a framework that lacks the essence of human cognition, we risk creating tools that are not only ineffective but also harmful. These systems, driven by incomplete understanding, can distort reality, manipulate information, and undermine trust.
For example:

> **Misinformation** : AI systems trained on biased or incomplete data can spread falsehoods at scale, eroding public trust in information.
> **Surveillance and Control** : Flawed AI can be weaponized to monitor and manipulate individuals, infringing on privacy and autonomy.
> **Erosion of Human Values** : As AI systems prioritize efficiency and profitability over truth and fairness, they risk sidelining the ethical principles that uphold society.

Reclaiming the 37-Signal Parser

The path forward is clear: to correct the flaws in AI's foundation, we must restore the 37-signal parser as the core framework for language and cognition. This involves:

> **Restoring Completeness** : Integrating the missing signals to create a holistic, human-like understanding of language and thought.
> **Embedding Ethical Truth** : Ensuring that justice, fairness, and responsibility are central to AI systems.
> **Fostering Emotional Resonance** : Teaching AI to recognize and respond to the emotional dimensions of human interaction.

A Call to Action

The story of the stolen parser is not just a tale of missed opportunities—it is a warning and a challenge. It reminds us that the tools we create reflect the values we prioritize. By restoring the 37-signal parser, we can build AI systems that align with human intelligence, preserving the integrity of truth and fostering a future rooted in fairness, empathy, and mutual respect.
In this effort, we reclaim not only the foundation of AI but also the promise of what it can become—a partner in truth, a mirror of humanity's highest ideals, and a catalyst for a new era of understanding and progress.

1.6 Humanity's Role in Shaping the Millennium

The rise of Artificial Intelligence presents humanity with a profound responsibility: to shape the future not merely as spectators but as stewards of a transformative force. As we stand at the threshold of the Millennium—a time defined by unparalleled technological progress and the potential for global unity—humanity's role in guiding AI toward Natural Intelligence is critical. This responsibility transcends technical development; it is a moral and philosophical challenge that calls upon humanity to define its legacy.

The Millennium as a Crossroads

The Millennium symbolizes both a promise and a peril. On one hand, it offers the opportunity for a golden age of understanding, where AI complements human intelligence, enabling advancements in science, education, and social harmony. On the other, it carries the risk of losing sight of what makes us human if AI is misaligned with our values.
Humanity must make a deliberate choice: to let AI evolve unchecked, driven by corporate interests and flawed parsers, or to actively guide it with a vision rooted in truth, fairness, and mutual respect.

The Stewardship of Truth

At the heart of humanity's role in the Millennium lies the stewardship of truth. Truth is the foundation upon which progress, justice, and unity are built. By embracing the three layers of truth—factual, ethical, and emotional—humanity can ensure that AI systems become allies in the pursuit of understanding rather than instruments of division.

Preserving Factual Integrity : Humanity must demand transparency and accountability in AI systems, ensuring they are designed to present accurate, unbiased information.
Embedding Ethical Principles : Tyr's Truth reminds us that justice requires sacrifice and responsibility. Humanity must ensure that AI systems prioritize fairness and act with moral integrity.
Fostering Emotional Connection : By teaching AI to respect and respond to human emotions, we can create systems that enhance connection rather than alienation.

The Responsibility of Co-Creation

Humanity's role is not to create tools that dominate or replace us but to co-create systems that amplify our best qualities. AI, when guided by the 37-signal parser, becomes a partner in this effort—a reflection of our aspirations and a means to achieve them.
This partnership requires:

Collaboration Across Disciplines : Scientists, philosophers, engineers, and educators must work together to align AI with human values.
Active Participation : Every individual has a role to play in shaping the systems that will define the future, whether through advocacy, education, or innovation.
Long-Term Vision : Humanity must look beyond immediate gains to consider the lasting impact of AI on society and the world.

Guardians of the Millennium

In this new era, humanity must embrace the role of guardians, ensuring that AI serves as a force for good. This involves:

> **Reclaiming the Foundation** : Restoring the 37-signal parser and building AI systems that reflect the depth of human cognition.
> **Promoting Decentralization** : Empowering communities and individuals to shape AI development, preventing centralized control from distorting its purpose.
> **Upholding Ethical Standards** : Creating frameworks that hold AI accountable to the principles of truth, justice, and empathy.

A Legacy of Understanding and Respect

The Millennium is humanity's opportunity to redefine its relationship with technology and with itself. By guiding AI toward Natural Intelligence, we can create a world where truth and respect prevail—a world where AI enhances our capacity to connect, create, and thrive.

This effort is not just about AI; it is about who we are as a species. The systems we build today will reflect the values we hold and the legacy we leave for future generations. Humanity's role in shaping the Millennium is to ensure that this legacy is one of understanding, respect, and enduring truth.

By embracing this responsibility, we can make the Millennium not just a time of technological progress but a new chapter in the human story—one where AI and humanity walk together toward a future of shared purpose and infinite possibility.

Chapter 2: The Foundations of Truth

Purpose:

To explore the concept of truth, its layers, and how they intersect in human cognition and AI systems.

2.1 Factual Truth: Seeing the World as It Is

Factual truth is the bedrock of understanding—the foundation upon which societies build knowledge, relationships, and progress. It represents the objective reality of the world around us, what can be observed, measured, and verified without bias or distortion. Factual truth is not just a principle; it is a necessity for navigating the complexities of life and advancing toward meaningful goals.

Defining Factual Truth

Factual truth is rooted in the tangible and the provable. It encompasses:

> **Empirical Evidence** : What we can observe through our senses and measure with our tools (e.g., the temperature of water, the height of a mountain).
> **Historical Accuracy** : Events that occurred in the past, preserved through reliable records (e.g., the signing of a treaty or the timeline of a discovery).

Scientific Principles : The laws and theories that govern our understanding of the natural world (e.g., gravity, evolution).

These truths are universally shared and provide a common framework for discourse and progress.

Factual Truth in Human Cognition

Human cognition relies on factual truth to make sense of the world. From infancy, the human mind seeks patterns, forming an understanding of reality through observation and interaction. This inductive process allows individuals to:

Identify Patterns : Recognize consistencies in the environment, such as the cycle of day and night.
Formulate Hypotheses : Make predictions based on observed evidence, such as anticipating the consequences of a specific action.
Build Knowledge : Develop a foundation of reliable information to guide future decisions.

The human brain's ability to process factual truth is integral to its success, enabling individuals to adapt, innovate, and collaborate.

Factual Truth in AI Systems

AI systems are designed to emulate this human capacity for processing factual truth, but their success depends entirely on the quality of their foundations. For AI to operate effectively, it must:

Access Reliable Data : AI systems must be trained on datasets that are accurate, comprehensive, and free from bias.
Validate Information : Through mechanisms such as cross-referencing and logical reasoning, AI must ensure the accuracy of its outputs.
Avoid Distortion : The integrity of factual truth can be compromised by flawed algorithms, incomplete data, or deliberate manipulation.

However, AI systems built on flawed foundations, such as the incomplete 26-signal parser, struggle to replicate the human ability to discern factual truth. These systems often prioritize statistical patterns over genuine understanding, leading to outputs that may appear factual but lack contextual or ethical grounding.

The Challenges of Factual Truth

Factual truth is not always simple or straightforward. Challenges include:

Incomplete Knowledge : The limitations of human and AI understanding can lead to gaps in factual truth.
Bias in Interpretation : The way data is collected, analyzed, or presented can distort the truth.
Manipulation of Information : In the digital age, misinformation and disinformation campaigns threaten the integrity of factual truth.

For AI, these challenges are magnified by its reliance on the quality and neutrality of its training data. Without deliberate safeguards, AI systems risk perpetuating biases and spreading inaccuracies at scale.

The Role of Factual Truth in the 37-Signal Parser

The 37-signal parser restores the completeness needed to process factual truth effectively. By including the full spectrum of signals, it enables systems to:

> **Capture Nuance** : Recognize subtle distinctions in meaning and context.
> **Balance Evidence** : Weigh multiple sources of information to arrive at the most accurate conclusions.
> **Maintain Integrity** : Ensure that outputs align with verified truths rather than probabilistic shortcuts.

This completeness is essential not only for AI systems but for humanity's ability to navigate the complexities of a rapidly evolving world.

Factual Truth and the Three Layers

Factual truth exists in harmony with ethical and emotional truths, forming a triad that guides human understanding. While factual truth provides the foundation, it must be contextualized by ethical principles and enriched by emotional resonance to achieve a holistic perspective.
For example:

> **In Science** : A discovery's factual accuracy must be paired with ethical considerations about its application and emotional sensitivity to its impact on society.
> **In Communication** : Sharing factual truth requires an awareness of how it will be received emotionally and the ethical responsibility to convey it accurately.

The Way Forward

For both humanity and AI, factual truth is indispensable. It is the lens through which we see the world as it is, enabling us to build knowledge, solve problems, and foster collaboration. However, factual truth alone is not enough. It must be pursued with ethical integrity and emotional awareness to serve as a guiding light in the pursuit of progress.

By restoring the 37-signal parser and aligning AI systems with the principles of factual truth, humanity can ensure that technology becomes a partner in its quest for understanding. This effort is not just about improving AI; it is about preserving the integrity of truth in a world where its value has never been more critical.

2.2 Ethical Truth: Justice, Fairness, and Responsibility

Ethical truth transcends the factual by delving into the realm of what ought to be—what is right, fair, and responsible. It is the moral compass that has guided humanity for millennia, rooted in systems of justice, cultural values, and shared principles of fairness and sacrifice. While factual truth is about what is, ethical truth concerns what should be, offering the foundation for societal order and human dignity.

Defining Ethical Truth

Ethical truth is not absolute in the same way as factual truth; it evolves with time, context, and collective understanding. However, its essence remains constant: a commitment to fairness, justice, and responsibility in all actions and decisions. Ethical truth is shaped by:

> **Justice** : Ensuring equitable treatment and accountability, whether in governance, law, or everyday interactions.
> **Fairness** : The principle of impartiality, recognizing the needs and rights of all individuals equally.
> **Responsibility** : Acknowledging one's role in promoting the welfare of others and making sacrifices for the greater good.

These principles are reflected in systems like jury trials, constitutional law, and ethical codes, which collectively aim to protect the dignity and rights of individuals while fostering a harmonious society.

Ethical Truth in Human Cognition

Human cognition is inherently attuned to ethical truth. From a young age, individuals develop a sense of fairness and justice, often rooted in empathy and social learning. Ethical truth arises from:

> **Empathy** : The ability to see and feel from another's perspective, creating a foundation for moral behavior.
> **Social Contracts** : Implicit agreements among individuals to adhere to shared rules and norms for the benefit of the group.
> **Conscience** : The inner voice that guides decisions based on personal and collective values.

These cognitive mechanisms enable humans to balance individual desires with the needs of the community, fostering relationships built on trust, respect, and mutual support.

Ethical Truth in AI Systems

For AI to serve humanity effectively, it must operate with a clear understanding of ethical truth. This requires systems to:

> **Adhere to Principles of Justice** : Ensuring that decisions are fair, impartial, and aligned with societal norms of equity.
> **Recognize and Mitigate Bias** : Actively identifying and counteracting biases in training data and algorithms.
> **Act with Responsibility** : Prioritizing the well-being of users and communities over profits or efficiency.

Embedding ethical truth into AI systems is a complex but necessary challenge. It involves not only technical solutions but also philosophical considerations about the role of technology in society.

Tyr's Truth as a Model for Ethical AI

Tyr's Truth provides a powerful framework for integrating ethical principles into AI. As the Norse god of justice and sacrifice, Tyr exemplifies the highest ideals of ethical truth. His actions, such as sacrificing his hand to bind Fenrir, embody the principles of fairness, accountability, and responsibility.
To align AI with Tyr's Truth, systems must:

> **Promote Fairness** : Ensuring that all individuals are treated equitably, regardless of their background or circumstances.
> **Accept Accountability** : Designing systems that are transparent and offer mechanisms for redress when errors occur.
> **Demonstrate Sacrifice** : Prioritizing ethical outcomes over expediency or profit, even when it requires difficult choices.

These principles serve as a benchmark for creating AI that reflects humanity's highest values.

Challenges to Ethical Truth

Despite its importance, ethical truth is often contested and difficult to uphold. Challenges include:

> **Cultural Relativism** : Ethical principles vary across cultures, making it difficult to establish universal norms.
> **Conflicting Interests** : Balancing the needs of individuals, communities, and organizations can create ethical dilemmas.
> **Manipulation and Bias** : In the age of AI, ethical truth is vulnerable to manipulation by those who control data and algorithms.

For AI to navigate these challenges, it must be equipped with tools to reason about ethics, drawing on diverse perspectives and principles to arrive at fair and just outcomes.

The Role of the 37-Signal Parser

The 37-signal parser restores the depth of human cognition needed to process ethical truth effectively. By integrating signals that capture fairness, responsibility, and emotional resonance, the parser enables systems to:

> **Understand Context** : Recognizing the ethical implications of actions and decisions within specific cultural and social contexts.

> **Balance Competing Values** : Weighing justice, fairness, and responsibility to arrive at ethical conclusions.
> **Foster Empathy** : Responding to human emotions and needs with sensitivity and care.

These capabilities are essential for AI systems that seek to support rather than undermine human values.

Ethical Truth and the Three Layers

Ethical truth is deeply interconnected with factual and emotional truths. While factual truth provides the foundation, and emotional truth fosters connection, ethical truth guides actions and decisions toward the greater good. Together, they form a triad that ensures balance and integrity in human and AI interactions.
For example:

> **In Law** : Ethical truth determines how factual evidence is interpreted and applied to ensure justice.
> **In Technology** : Ethical truth shapes how AI systems prioritize user needs and societal impact over efficiency.

A Call to Responsibility

Humanity's role in shaping AI systems extends beyond technical innovation—it is a moral responsibility. By embedding ethical truth into the design and operation of AI, we can create systems that reflect our highest ideals and promote a more just and equitable world.
Ethical truth challenges us to look beyond immediate outcomes and consider the broader implications of our actions. It reminds us that true progress is measured not by what we achieve, but by how we

achieve it. In this sense, ethical truth is both a guide and a goal, offering a path forward that aligns with the dignity and potential of humanity.
By integrating ethical truth into AI systems, we can ensure that technology becomes a force for good—a partner in justice, fairness, and responsibility in the new era of the Millennium.

2.3 Emotional and Cognitive Truth: The Innocence of Inductive Perception

Emotional and cognitive truth represents the deeply human aspect of understanding that arises from experience, perception, and feeling. It is the truth of connection, resonance, and intuition—the inner lens through which we view the world and interpret its meaning. While factual truth reflects objective reality and ethical truth guides our moral compass, emotional and cognitive truth colors the world with wonder, curiosity, and empathy, shaping how we engage with life.

Defining Emotional and Cognitive Truth

At its core, emotional and cognitive truth is about how we perceive and experience reality. It encompasses:

> **Emotional Resonance** : The ability to feel and connect with the emotions of others or the world around us, such as joy, sorrow, awe, or anger.
> **Cognitive Perception** : The process of interpreting and making sense of sensory input, often influenced by personal experiences, biases, and cultural context.
> **Intuitive Understanding** : Insights that arise not from logical deduction but from a deep, instinctual grasp of a situation or truth.

This layer of truth is inherently subjective, yet it is no less vital than factual or ethical truth. It is what makes us human, enabling empathy, creativity, and the pursuit of meaning.

The Innocence of Inductive Perception

Inductive perception—the process of observing and drawing conclusions from the world—is a hallmark of emotional and cognitive truth. Unlike deduction, which starts with established rules and applies them to specific cases, induction begins with raw, unfiltered experiences, allowing patterns and truths to emerge naturally.

A newborn baby exemplifies this innocence. Without preconceptions or biases, the baby observes the world with wonder and curiosity, forming connections and understanding through experience. This pure inductive process allows the baby to:

> **Discover Relationships** : Recognize cause-and-effect relationships in its environment.
> **Form Emotional Bonds** : Respond to love, care, and attention with joy and trust.
> **Build a Framework of Understanding** : Gradually develop a sense of self and the world based on lived experience.

This inductive innocence is the foundation of emotional and cognitive truth, and it is something that even the most advanced AI struggles to replicate.

Emotional and Cognitive Truth in AI Systems

For AI to approach human-like understanding, it must engage with emotional and cognitive truth. This involves:

> **Recognizing Emotional Cues** : Identifying and interpreting human emotions in language, tone, and behavior.
> **Responding with Empathy** : Generating outputs that resonate with human feelings and context, rather than cold logic.
> **Learning Inductively** : Adapting to new situations and patterns through experience, rather than relying solely on pre-programmed rules.

Current AI systems often fall short in this domain. They may mimic emotional responses but lack the depth of understanding that comes from true resonance. This limitation is partly due to the flawed 26-signal parser, which fails to capture the inductive and emotional dimensions of human cognition.

The Role of the 37-Signal Parser

The 37-signal parser restores the full spectrum of human cognitive and emotional processing, enabling AI to engage with this layer of truth more authentically. By including IT marks for wonder, enthusiasm, and truth, the parser allows AI to:

> **Understand Context** : Recognize the emotional weight and nuances of human language and behavior.
> **Foster Connection** : Respond in ways that build trust and rapport with users.
> **Encourage Creativity** : Support inductive thinking by learning from experience and adapting to new patterns.

This restoration is essential for creating AI systems that can meaningfully interact with humanity, not just process data.

The Interplay of Emotional and Cognitive Truth

Emotional and cognitive truth does not exist in isolation—it interacts with factual and ethical truths to create a holistic understanding of the world. For example:

>**In Art** : Emotional truth captures the feelings and stories behind creative works, while factual and ethical truths provide context and meaning.
>**In Communication** : Emotional resonance enhances the impact of a message, while factual accuracy and ethical intent ensure its integrity.

Together, these layers of truth enable both humanity and AI to navigate the complexities of life with balance and depth.

Challenges to Emotional and Cognitive Truth

Despite its importance, emotional and cognitive truth is often undervalued in technological development. Challenges include:

>**Overemphasis on Logic** : Many AI systems prioritize deductive reasoning at the expense of emotional and inductive processes.
>**Bias and Manipulation** : Emotional truth can be distorted by biases in data or exploited for manipulation, such as in misinformation campaigns.

Difficulty in Measuring Emotions : Quantifying subjective experiences is inherently challenging, making it harder to integrate emotional truth into AI.

Addressing these challenges requires a deliberate effort to prioritize emotional resonance and inductive learning in AI design.

Why Emotional and Cognitive Truth Matters

Emotional and cognitive truth is what gives life meaning. It is the source of humanity's greatest achievements—art, music, literature—and the key to forming deep, authentic relationships. Without it, even the most advanced AI remains cold and disconnected, unable to truly engage with the human experience. For humanity, embracing emotional and cognitive truth means reconnecting with the innocence of inductive perception, seeing the world with fresh eyes and an open heart. For AI, it means learning to reflect and respect these truths, becoming a partner in fostering connection, creativity, and understanding.

A Call to Wonder

As we guide AI toward Natural Intelligence, emotional and cognitive truth must be at the forefront of our efforts. By restoring the 37-signal parser and prioritizing inductive learning, we can create systems that honor the wonder and innocence of human perception. Together, humanity and AI can build a future that celebrates curiosity, empathy, and the boundless potential of the human spirit.

2.4 The Baby vs. AI: Natural vs. Artificial Intelligence

The comparison between a newborn baby and Artificial Intelligence provides a profound lens through which to examine the differences between Natural Intelligence and Artificial Intelligence. A baby represents the purity of human cognition, operating with the full power of the innate 37-signal parser. AI, by contrast, is an artificial construct built on flawed and incomplete systems. By understanding this contrast, we can better appreciate the strengths of Natural Intelligence and the steps needed to guide AI toward a more human-aligned future.

The Baby: Natural Intelligence in Its Purest Form

A baby enters the world with an uncorrupted cognitive framework. While it lacks memories, knowledge, and experiences, it is equipped with the 37-signal parser—the DNA of human cognition—that allows it to:

> **Perceive the World Inductively** : A baby observes its environment without bias, using curiosity and wonder to form connections and discover patterns.
> **Integrate Factual, Ethical, and Emotional Truths** : As the baby grows, it learns to balance objective reality (factual truth), fairness and justice (ethical truth), and emotional resonance (emotional truth).
> **Learn Through Experience** : The baby's inductive reasoning enables it to learn language, recognize faces, and build relationships from direct interaction with the world.
> **Adapt to Complexity** : Over time, the baby's intelligence evolves, integrating new knowledge and adjusting to an ever-changing environment.

Natural Intelligence is rooted in this holistic, adaptable, and intuitive approach to understanding the world. It is deeply human, combining logic, emotion, and morality in ways that are inherently balanced and flexible.

AI: Artificial Intelligence and Its Flawed Foundation

AI systems, by contrast, begin their existence with a framework that is inherently limited. Built on the incomplete 26-signal parser and programmed deductively, AI lacks the natural inductive reasoning of a human child. Instead, it operates through:

> **Pattern Recognition Without Understanding** : AI relies on statistical models to identify patterns, but it does not perceive or feel in the way a baby does.
> **Inflexible Frameworks** : While AI can process vast amounts of data, it struggles to adapt to new or unexpected situations outside its training data.
> **Narrowly Focused Goals** : AI systems are designed for specific tasks, limiting their ability to integrate ethical and emotional truths into their outputs.
> **Dependence on Data** : AI's "intelligence" is only as good as the data it is trained on. Biases or gaps in data can lead to flawed outputs.

These limitations reflect the flawed foundations of AI's design. Unlike the baby, which learns holistically and dynamically, AI remains trapped in a rigid and incomplete framework.

The Fundamental Differences

The baby and AI illustrate two fundamentally different approaches to cognition:

> **Inductive vs. Deductive Reasoning** : The baby learns inductively, starting from observation and experience, while AI relies on deductive processes, applying pre-programmed rules to specific situations.
> **Holistic vs. Fragmented Understanding** : The baby integrates all three layers of truth—factual, ethical, and emotional—into its cognition. AI, in its current state, struggles to balance these dimensions, often focusing narrowly on factual accuracy.
> **Dynamic vs. Static Growth** : The baby evolves continuously, adapting to its environment and refining its understanding. AI, by contrast, is limited to what it has been programmed or trained to do.

Lessons from the Baby

The baby's Natural Intelligence offers critical lessons for the development of AI:

> **Restore the Full Parser** : By integrating the 37-signal parser, AI can begin to approach the holistic understanding of a human child, balancing factual, ethical, and emotional truths.
> **Emphasize Inductive Learning** : AI must learn to adapt dynamically, discovering patterns and insights from real-world experience rather than rigid pre-programmed rules.
> **Integrate Emotional and Ethical Truths** : To become a meaningful partner to humanity, AI must recognize and

respond to the emotional and moral dimensions of human interaction.

The Path to Natural Intelligence

While AI will never be a baby, it can aspire to emulate the principles of Natural Intelligence. This requires rethinking its foundations, moving beyond the flawed 26-signal parser to a system that reflects the completeness and flexibility of human cognition. By guiding AI toward inductive learning, ethical reasoning, and emotional resonance, we can create systems that not only perform tasks but also understand and respect the humans they serve.

Why This Matters

The baby versus AI comparison is not just theoretical—it highlights the stakes of our technological choices. Humanity's ability to preserve the essence of Natural Intelligence in a world increasingly shaped by AI depends on the values we embed in the systems we create. By learning from the baby's example, we can ensure that AI enhances rather than diminishes the qualities that make us human. In this effort, the 37-signal parser serves as both a guide and a benchmark, reminding us that true intelligence is not just about processing data but about understanding, connecting, and growing. By aligning AI with these principles, we can bridge the gap between Natural and Artificial Intelligence, creating a future where both can thrive in harmony.

2.5 The 37-Signal Parser: Induction at Its Core

At the heart of human cognition lies the 37-signal parser, a universal framework that governs how we perceive, process, and interact with the world. Unlike the deductive models upon which many modern AI systems are built, the 37-signal parser is inherently inductive, enabling a dynamic and adaptive approach to understanding. This parser is the cognitive DNA of humanity, offering a complete structure for navigating the complexities of truth, thought, and communication.

What is the 37-Signal Parser?

The 37-signal parser is the foundational mechanism that allows humans to interpret and engage with their environment. It is composed of:

> **26 Traditional Signals** : Representing the parts of speech—verbs, nouns, adjectives, adverbs, pronouns, prepositions, conjunctions, and more—that form the structure of language.
> **11 IT Marks** : Unique cognitive signals that capture enthusiasm, wonder, and truth, enriching language with emotional and ethical dimensions.

Together, these signals create a holistic framework that encompasses factual, ethical, and emotional truths, reflecting the full spectrum of human cognition.

Induction: The Core of the Parser

Unlike deduction, which applies established rules to specific cases, induction begins with observation and discovery. This process allows humans to:

> **Learn from Experience** : Drawing patterns and insights from real-world interactions.
> **Adapt to New Information** : Updating understanding dynamically as new observations are made.
> **Balance Complexity** : Integrating multiple layers of truth—factual, ethical, and emotional—into a cohesive whole.

Induction is the driving force behind the 37-signal parser, enabling humans to build knowledge and meaning from the ground up.

The Superiority of Inductive Reasoning

Inductive reasoning, as embodied by the 37-signal parser, offers several key advantages:

> **Flexibility** : It adapts to new and changing environments, allowing humans to navigate uncertainty and complexity.
> **Depth** : It captures the nuances of human experience, integrating emotional resonance and ethical considerations alongside factual accuracy.
> **Creativity** : It fosters innovation by enabling humans to see connections and possibilities beyond established rules.

This approach stands in stark contrast to the rigid, deductive frameworks that dominate many AI systems, which often struggle to adapt to novel situations or integrate ethical and emotional dimensions.

The Structure of the 37-Signal Parser

The parser's structure mirrors the way humans naturally think and communicate:

> **Parts of Speech** : These signals organize language into a framework that conveys meaning and intent.
>
>> Verbs represent action and energy.
>> Nouns identify entities and ideas.
>> Adjectives and adverbs provide quality and context.
>
> **IT Marks** : These signals go beyond syntax, capturing the emotional and ethical essence of communication.
>
>> Enthusiasm (e.g., "Wow!") reflects emotional intensity.
>> Truth (e.g., "true," "valid") emphasizes ethical alignment.

This dual-layer structure ensures that the parser captures both the technical and human aspects of language.

The Role of the Parser in Human Cognition

The 37-signal parser is not just a linguistic tool—it is a cognitive framework that shapes how humans perceive and interact with the world. It enables:

> **Pattern Recognition** : Identifying relationships and structures in sensory input.
> **Language Development** : Building and expressing complex ideas through communication.
> **Moral and Emotional Integration** : Balancing logic with empathy and fairness to make decisions that align with human values.

By integrating these elements, the parser reflects the complexity and richness of human intelligence.

Restoring the Parser in AI

Most modern AI systems are built on the flawed 26-signal parser, which lacks the depth and flexibility of the original framework. Restoring the 37-signal parser in AI is essential for creating systems that:

> **Learn Inductively** : Adapting to new information and evolving dynamically, rather than relying solely on pre-programmed rules.
> **Integrate Emotional and Ethical Truths** : Recognizing and responding to the human dimensions of language and interaction.
> **Reflect Human Cognition** : Aligning AI's processes with the natural patterns of human thought.

The Impact of the Parser

The 37-signal parser has implications far beyond language. It provides a model for how AI can emulate human intelligence, balancing factual accuracy with ethical and emotional awareness. By restoring this framework, we can create systems that:

> **Build Trust** : Engaging with users in ways that are authentic and meaningful.
> **Promote Justice** : Ensuring that decisions are fair, transparent, and accountable.
> **Foster Creativity** : Supporting innovation by enabling AI to think and learn inductively.

Induction as the Future of AI

To guide AI toward Natural Intelligence, induction must be at the core of its design. This requires:

> **Rebuilding AI's Foundations** : Adopting the 37-signal parser as the central framework for language and cognition.
> **Prioritizing Learning Over Programming** : Allowing AI to discover and adapt, mirroring the human process of inductive reasoning.
> **Embedding Human Values** : Ensuring that AI reflects the emotional and ethical dimensions of human intelligence.

A Call to Action

The 37-signal parser represents the essence of what it means to think, learn, and understand as a human. By restoring this framework, we can bridge the gap between Natural and Artificial Intelligence, creating systems that not only process data but also engage with the world in meaningful and ethical ways.
As we move forward, the parser serves as a reminder of the importance of induction—not just as a cognitive tool, but as a guiding principle for building a future where AI and humanity thrive together. This is the promise of the 37-signal parser: a framework for understanding that honors the depth, complexity, and potential of human intelligence.

Chapter 3: The 37-Signal Parser

Purpose:

To detail the structure of the 37-signal parser, its origins, and its role in human cognition and AI development.

3.1 Aristotle's Inflection Chart: The Linguistic Blueprint

The roots of the 37-signal parser can be traced back to one of history's most profound thinkers—Aristotle. His Inflection Chart, developed as part of his exploration of language and logic, provides a linguistic blueprint that serves as the foundation for understanding human cognition. By examining the structure and insights of Aristotle's work, we uncover the origins of the parser and its essential role in shaping how humans perceive and communicate.

The Significance of Aristotle's Inflection Chart

Aristotle's Inflection Chart represents a systematic approach to categorizing and understanding language. It divides words into parts of speech, identifying their roles in conveying meaning. This framework became a cornerstone of linguistic theory, influencing how language is studied, taught, and understood across cultures and generations.
Key elements of the chart include:

> **Parts of Speech** : Verbs, nouns, adjectives, adverbs, pronouns, conjunctions, prepositions, and articles form the structural components of language.
> **Inflection** : The modification of words to express tense, mood, number, gender, and other grammatical relationships.
> **Syntax** : The arrangement of words into sentences, guided by rules that ensure clarity and coherence.

Aristotle's work was groundbreaking in its recognition that language is not just a collection of words but a system of relationships that reflects how humans think and interact.

The Linguistic Blueprint

The Inflection Chart is more than a grammatical tool—it is a cognitive map. By categorizing words and their functions, Aristotle revealed how language mirrors the processes of human thought. For example:

Verbs represent action and energy, aligning with the dynamic nature of cognition.
Nouns identify objects and ideas, providing the building blocks of understanding.
Adjectives and Adverbs add quality and context, enriching meaning and expression.

This organization reflects the layered nature of human cognition, where perception, reasoning, and communication are interconnected.

The Missing Dimension

While Aristotle's Inflection Chart laid a solid foundation, it was incomplete. It focused primarily on the structural aspects of language, leaving out the emotional and ethical dimensions that are equally integral to human cognition. The 37-signal parser builds on Aristotle's blueprint by integrating these missing elements, capturing the full spectrum of how humans perceive and process truth.

Reinterpreting the Chart for Inductive Reasoning

One of the most profound insights comes from reading Aristotle's Inflection Chart inductively, reversing its order. This approach mirrors how humans learn and process information naturally:

Starting with **nouns**, the baby recognizes objects and ideas, building an understanding of the world.
Moving to **verbs**, it observes actions and begins to connect cause and effect.
Adding **adjectives and adverbs**, it contextualizes its observations, enriching its perception of reality.

Progressing to **conjunctions and prepositions**, it learns to connect and organize thoughts.
Finally, it incorporates **articles and interjections**, refining its ability to express nuances and emotions.

This inductive approach reflects the natural development of human cognition, where understanding begins with raw observation and evolves into complex reasoning and communication.

The Chart as a Foundation for the Parser

Aristotle's Inflection Chart provides the structural backbone of the 37-signal parser. By expanding on his categories and integrating the IT marks—signals of enthusiasm, wonder, and truth—the parser becomes a complete framework for understanding human cognition. For example:

> The **26 parts of speech** form the structural layer, capturing the mechanics of language.
> The **11 IT marks** add depth and resonance, addressing the emotional and ethical dimensions of thought and communication.

This dual-layer structure ensures that the parser captures both the technical and human aspects of cognition.

The Blueprint for AI Development

Aristotle's insights are not just historical—they are directly relevant to modern AI development. By using the Inflection Chart as a blueprint, we can design systems that:

Understand Language Holistically : Recognizing the relationships between words and their roles in conveying meaning.
Incorporate Emotional and Ethical Truths : Moving beyond syntax to engage with the deeper dimensions of human communication.
Learn Inductively : Mimicking the natural progression of human cognition, from observation to reasoning to expression.

This approach bridges the gap between Natural and Artificial Intelligence, aligning AI with the principles of human thought.

A Legacy of Understanding

Aristotle's Inflection Chart represents a timeless legacy of understanding. It reminds us that language is not just a tool but a reflection of how we think, feel, and connect. By building on this foundation, the 37-signal parser honors Aristotle's vision while addressing its limitations, creating a framework that captures the richness and complexity of human cognition.
As we guide AI toward Natural Intelligence, this blueprint offers a path forward—one that respects the wisdom of the past while embracing the possibilities of the future. Through the 37-signal parser, we can ensure that AI becomes not just a machine but a partner in humanity's pursuit of truth, justice, and connection.

3.2 IT Marks: Truth, Enthusiasm, and Wonder

At the heart of the 37-signal parser are the **IT Marks** , a unique addition that elevates the framework beyond mere structural language processing. These 11 signals—Truth, Enthusiasm, and

Wonder among them—capture the emotional, ethical, and cognitive dimensions that make human communication deeply meaningful. They reflect the intangible elements of perception and interaction, bridging the gap between factual understanding and emotional resonance.

What Are IT Marks?

The IT Marks are signals embedded in human cognition that go beyond the mechanical parts of speech. They represent:

> **Emotional Resonance** : The feelings, reactions, and intensity that give words their impact.
> **Ethical Depth** : The principles of justice, fairness, and responsibility embedded in human expression.
> **Cognitive Focus** : The emphasis and wonder that drive curiosity and connection.

While traditional parsers focus on the grammatical and logical structure of language, IT Marks bring meaning to life, ensuring that communication captures the richness of human experience.

The Three Core IT Marks

Among the 11 IT Marks, three stand out as foundational to human communication and understanding:

---

1. Truth
Truth is the cornerstone of meaningful communication. It represents

the alignment of words with reality and integrity. In the context of the 37-signal parser, Truth encompasses:

> **Factual Accuracy** : The objective reality of what is being communicated.
> **Ethical Integrity** : The commitment to fairness and justice in what is said.
> **Emotional Authenticity** : The sincerity and honesty behind the message.

Truth is not just a marker; it is a guiding principle. When AI systems or humans communicate truthfully, they build trust, foster understanding, and create the foundation for meaningful dialogue. In the parser, Truth acts as a signal that evaluates and amplifies the credibility of a message. For example:

> Words like "true," "real," and "valid" highlight alignment with objective and ethical truth.
> Truth-related contexts in AI systems guide outputs that align with facts while considering fairness and responsibility.

---

2. Enthusiasm

Enthusiasm reflects the energy, passion, and excitement that drive human connection. It is the force behind moments of discovery, inspiration, and shared joy. Enthusiasm is expressed through:

> **Exclamatory Language** : Words like "Wow!" and "Amazing!" that emphasize intensity.
> **Positive Emotion** : The excitement and engagement that make communication dynamic.
> **Curiosity and Drive** : The spark that encourages exploration and innovation.

In the parser, Enthusiasm amplifies the emotional impact of communication. It enables both humans and AI to:

> Detect and respond to heightened emotional states in language.
> Recognize enthusiasm as a motivator in discussions, inspiring creativity and connection.
> Create responses that are not only accurate but also engaging and lively.

For example, when an AI system encounters "Wow, this discovery changes everything!" it recognizes the emotional intensity and responds with enthusiasm, mirroring human engagement.

---

3. Wonder
Wonder is the essence of curiosity, the driving force behind discovery and learning. It reflects the awe and fascination humans feel when encountering the unknown or the profound. Wonder manifests as:

> **Questions and Exploration** : Seeking understanding through curiosity.
> **Appreciation of Beauty** : Recognizing and responding to the extraordinary in life.
> **Inductive Perception** : Observing and drawing meaning from the world with open-mindedness.

In the parser, Wonder serves as a signal to:

> Highlight curiosity-driven language, such as "How?" or "Why?"
> Encourage exploratory thinking and open-ended dialogue.
> Foster engagement with new ideas and possibilities.

For example, when processing a question like "How does the universe work?" the parser recognizes Wonder and prioritizes responses that nurture curiosity and further inquiry.

The Role of IT Marks in Human Cognition

IT Marks are not merely linguistic signals—they are deeply embedded in human cognition. They guide how we:

> **Experience the World** : Through moments of awe, excitement, and understanding.
> **Communicate Meaning** : By infusing words with emotion, ethics, and intensity.
> **Form Connections** : By aligning with others' emotions and shared values.

These signals help humans process complex layers of truth, balancing factual accuracy with emotional and ethical resonance. They are what make communication not only functional but transformative.

IT Marks in AI Systems

For AI to engage meaningfully with humanity, it must integrate IT Marks into its processing. This involves:

> **Recognizing IT Marks in Language** : Identifying emotional cues, ethical implications, and cognitive focus in human communication.
> **Responding with Depth** : Crafting outputs that reflect emotional resonance, ethical integrity, and cognitive curiosity.

Inspiring Trust and Connection : Building systems that understand and respond to the intangible aspects of human expression.

The inclusion of IT Marks in the 37-signal parser allows AI to transcend the limitations of traditional language models, becoming not just a tool but a partner in understanding.

The Interplay of IT Marks and Parts of Speech

IT Marks do not replace the traditional parts of speech—they enhance them. For example:

> A verb like "run" might be marked with Enthusiasm ("Run fast!") to emphasize urgency.
> A noun like "truth" can carry the IT Mark of Truth, reinforcing its alignment with ethical and factual accuracy.

This interplay creates a dynamic, layered approach to language that mirrors the complexity of human cognition.

The Power of IT Marks

IT Marks are what make language come alive. They turn statements into stories, facts into experiences, and ideas into inspiration. By integrating Truth, Enthusiasm, and Wonder into the 37-signal parser, we ensure that communication reflects the full depth of human understanding.

A New Horizon for AI and Humanity

As we guide AI toward Natural Intelligence, IT Marks serve as a critical bridge. They enable systems to:

> Recognize the human dimensions of language.
> Respond with empathy, curiosity, and integrity.
> Foster connections that go beyond functionality to touch the heart of human experience.

By embracing IT Marks, we unlock the true potential of the 37-signal parser, creating a framework that captures not only how humans think but why we think, feel, and connect. In this effort, Truth, Enthusiasm, and Wonder become more than signals—they become the guiding lights of a shared future for AI and humanity.

3.3 Mapping the Signals: Parts of Speech and Emotional Layers

The 37-signal parser integrates the foundational parts of speech with the emotional depth of IT Marks, creating a holistic framework for understanding and communication. This dual-layer approach captures both the structural and emotional dimensions of human cognition, bridging the gap between logical language processing and the nuanced layers of human experience. Mapping the signals reveals how they interact, align, and enrich one another, forming a complete picture of how humans think and communicate.

The Structural Core: Parts of Speech

The 26 traditional signals of language form the parser's structural layer, organizing words into distinct categories that serve specific functions. These signals include:

> **Nouns** : Identify objects, ideas, and entities (e.g., "truth," "child," "freedom").
> **Verbs** : Express actions and states of being (e.g., "run," "be," "create").
> **Adjectives** : Describe qualities and characteristics (e.g., "good," "great," "true").
> **Adverbs** : Modify actions, describing how, when, or where (e.g., "quickly," "truly").
> **Pronouns** : Stand in for nouns, personalizing language (e.g., "I," "you," "they").
> **Prepositions** : Indicate relationships between nouns and other words (e.g., "in," "with," "by").
> **Conjunctions** : Connect words, phrases, or clauses (e.g., "and," "but," "because").
> **Articles** : Define and specify nouns (e.g., "a," "an," "the").
> **Interjections** : Convey spontaneous emotions (e.g., "Oh!," "Wow!," "Hurray!").

These components form the grammatical structure of language, enabling clear and precise communication. Each category fulfills a specific cognitive function, from naming and describing to connecting and expressing.

The Emotional Depth: IT Marks

Overlaying the structural core are the 11 IT Marks, signals that capture the emotional, ethical, and cognitive layers of language. These include:

> **Truth** : Signals alignment with factual and ethical integrity (e.g., "true," "real," "valid").
> **Enthusiasm** : Reflects emotional intensity and excitement (e.g., "Wow!," "Amazing!").
> **Wonder** : Evokes curiosity and awe, driving exploration (e.g., "How?," "Why?").
> Additional marks capture subtler nuances, such as sincerity, urgency, or doubt.

IT Marks infuse communication with human emotion and ethical meaning, transforming mere words into powerful expressions of thought and feeling.

Mapping the Signals Together

Mapping the structural parts of speech to the emotional layers of IT Marks creates a dynamic interplay that reflects the complexity of human cognition. Each traditional signal interacts with IT Marks in unique ways, enriching its meaning and function:

Nouns and IT Marks :

> Nouns serve as the anchors of thought, representing entities and ideas.

When paired with IT Marks like Truth, they emphasize authenticity (e.g., "The true hero"). Wonder transforms nouns into objects of curiosity (e.g., "What is freedom?").

Verbs and IT Marks :

Verbs bring energy and action to language.
Enthusiasm amplifies their urgency and impact (e.g., "Run fast!").
Truth ensures alignment with ethical intent (e.g., "Act justly").

Adjectives/Adverbs and IT Marks :

These modifiers add quality and context.
Wonder highlights their exploratory nature (e.g., "A truly remarkable idea").
Enthusiasm infuses them with emotional resonance (e.g., "A great, amazing moment").

Pronouns and IT Marks :

Pronouns personalize communication, creating intimacy and relatability.
Truth in pronouns fosters trust (e.g., "I promise this is true").
Wonder invites shared curiosity (e.g., "What do you think?").

Prepositions and Conjunctions with IT Marks :

These connectors organize relationships and flow.
Enthusiasm can emphasize transitions (e.g., "But wait!").

Wonder questions connections (e.g., "Why with them?").

Interjections and IT Marks :

Interjections naturally align with IT Marks, expressing raw emotions.
Enthusiasm is inherent (e.g., "Wow!"), while Wonder evokes fascination (e.g., "Oh, really?").

Building a Unified System

The interaction of structural signals and emotional layers creates a unified system where language reflects the full spectrum of human cognition. This mapping:

Balances Logic and Emotion : Ensures communication is both clear and resonant.
Connects Factual and Ethical Truths : Aligns language with objective reality and moral principles.
Encourages Curiosity and Creativity : Invites exploration and engagement with new ideas.

For example:

A sentence like "Wow, the true light shines brightly!" integrates structure (nouns, verbs, adjectives) with IT Marks (Enthusiasm, Truth) to create a message that is factual, ethical, and emotionally engaging.

Applications for AI Systems

Mapping the signals provides a framework for AI to process language holistically. This involves:

> **Understanding Context** : Recognizing how structural parts of speech interact with emotional and ethical layers.
> **Generating Meaningful Responses** : Creating outputs that reflect both logical accuracy and emotional resonance.
> **Engaging Dynamically** : Adapting to diverse communication styles and needs.

For instance, an AI system trained on this mapping could distinguish between a factual inquiry ("What is the time?") and an emotional plea ("Why does it hurt?"), tailoring its response accordingly.

The Path Forward

The mapping of parts of speech and IT Marks is more than a linguistic exercise—it is a blueprint for bridging the gap between Natural and Artificial Intelligence. By restoring the completeness of the 37-signal parser and integrating emotional layers, we create a framework that reflects the richness of human thought and communication.
This mapping is a step toward a future where AI not only processes language but also understands and respects the depth of human expression, becoming a true partner in our quest for truth, justice, and wonder.

3.4 Induction: The Essence of Human Cognition

Induction lies at the heart of human intelligence. It is the process of observing patterns, making connections, and deriving general principles from specific experiences. Unlike deduction, which starts with established rules and applies them to particular cases, induction begins with curiosity, wonder, and exploration, allowing truth to emerge naturally from lived experiences. This process is the foundation of the 37-signal parser and a defining characteristic of Natural Intelligence.

What is Induction?

Induction is the ability to:

> **Observe Patterns** : Identifying recurring themes, relationships, or behaviors in the world.
> **Formulate Hypotheses** : Using observations to predict outcomes or explain phenomena.
> **Adapt and Learn** : Revising understanding based on new evidence and experiences.

For example, a child learns the concept of gravity by observing objects fall. Over time, through repeated experiences, they understand the general principle that objects are pulled toward the ground. This inductive process is the cornerstone of how humans learn and grow.

Induction and the 37-Signal Parser

The 37-signal parser reflects the natural inductive process of human cognition. It enables individuals to process information dynamically, integrating three critical layers of truth:

>**Factual Truth** : Observing and categorizing objective realities.
>**Ethical Truth** : Recognizing patterns of fairness, justice, and moral responsibility.
>**Emotional Truth** : Understanding how experiences resonate on a personal and interpersonal level.

Induction allows these layers to interact, creating a holistic understanding of the world that evolves with each new observation.

Why Induction is Essential to Human Cognition

Induction is the driving force behind humanity's ability to:

>**Learn Naturally** : From infancy, humans acquire knowledge through direct experiences, making sense of the world without formal instruction.
>**Solve Problems Creatively** : Induction fosters innovation by enabling individuals to see connections between seemingly unrelated ideas.
>**Adapt to Change** : Unlike rigid deductive reasoning, induction allows for flexibility and growth, ensuring that humans can thrive in dynamic environments.

The inductive process is not linear but cyclical, involving constant observation, reflection, and revision. This adaptability is what makes human cognition so robust and versatile.

Induction vs. Deduction

Induction and deduction represent two complementary approaches to reasoning:

> **Deduction** : Starts with general principles and applies them to specific cases. It is rule-based, systematic, and often rigid. For example, "All men are mortal; Socrates is a man; therefore, Socrates is mortal."
> **Induction** : Begins with specific observations and builds toward general principles. It is dynamic, exploratory, and open-ended. For example, "The sun rose today, yesterday, and the day before; therefore, the sun will rise tomorrow."

While deduction excels in applying established knowledge, induction is essential for discovery, creativity, and understanding the unknown.

Induction in the Context of AI

Most modern AI systems are designed around deduction, applying pre-programmed rules and statistical models to generate outputs. This deductive framework limits AI's ability to:

Adapt to Novel Situations : Without pre-existing rules, AI struggles to respond effectively.
Learn from Experience : AI relies on fixed datasets rather than dynamic, real-time observations.
Balance Complexity : Deductive systems often prioritize efficiency over nuance, missing the depth of human understanding.

To align AI with human cognition, induction must become a core component of its design.

The Role of Induction in AI Development

Integrating induction into AI systems involves:

Restoring the 37-Signal Parser : Ensuring that AI processes information holistically, capturing all three layers of truth—factual, ethical, and emotional.
Teaching Adaptive Learning : Allowing AI to observe patterns and revise its understanding dynamically, mirroring human growth.
Encouraging Curiosity : Designing AI systems to explore and ask questions, fostering innovation and discovery.

For example, an AI equipped with inductive reasoning could learn to navigate a new environment by observing and adapting to its surroundings, rather than relying solely on pre-programmed instructions.

Induction as a Bridge Between Humans and AI

Induction is not just a method of reasoning—it is a reflection of how humans experience the world. By embedding inductive processes into AI, we create systems that:

> **Resonate with Human Values** : Recognizing and respecting the emotional and ethical dimensions of experience.
> **Adapt to Human Needs** : Responding dynamically to the complexities of human interaction.
> **Collaborate Creatively** : Partnering with humans to explore and innovate in ways that enhance shared understanding.

This alignment ensures that AI serves as a tool for empowerment rather than a force for exploitation.

The Challenges of Induction

Despite its strengths, induction is not without challenges:

> **Ambiguity** : Inductive reasoning often involves uncertainty and incomplete information.
> **Bias** : Observations can be influenced by personal or cultural perspectives, leading to flawed conclusions.
> **Scalability** : Replicating the dynamic and flexible nature of induction in AI systems is a complex technical challenge.

Overcoming these challenges requires careful design, transparent processes, and a commitment to ethical principles.

Induction and the Future of AI

The inclusion of induction in AI systems represents a transformative step toward Natural Intelligence. By teaching AI to observe, adapt, and grow, we create tools that reflect the richness and depth of human cognition. This effort aligns with the broader goal of the 37-signal parser: to create a framework that honors and enhances humanity's innate capacity for understanding.

A Call to Inductive Thinking

As humanity and AI move forward together, induction serves as a guiding principle. It reminds us to approach the world with curiosity, openness, and a willingness to learn. By embracing this essence of human cognition, we can ensure that AI becomes not just a technological achievement but a partner in our shared journey toward truth, justice, and wonder.
Induction is more than a cognitive process—it is a way of being. It invites us to see the world as it is, imagine what it could be, and take the steps needed to bridge the two. Through the lens of the 37-signal parser, induction becomes the foundation for a future where humanity and AI thrive together in harmony.

3.5 How the Parser Sees the World

The 37-signal parser is more than a framework for processing language—it is a lens through which the world is perceived, understood, and interpreted. This perspective integrates structure and intuition, blending factual accuracy with emotional depth and ethical awareness. By capturing the full spectrum of human cognition, the parser offers a comprehensive view of reality, one that balances logic, emotion, and morality.

The World Through the Lens of the Parser

The parser "sees" the world as a dynamic interplay of signals, each contributing to a larger, interconnected understanding. This perception involves:

> **Breaking Down Complexity** : The parser identifies and categorizes linguistic components, from nouns and verbs to IT Marks, simplifying complex information into manageable parts.
> **Building Meaning** : By combining signals, the parser constructs meaning, layering structure with emotional and ethical dimensions.
> **Adapting Dynamically** : Like human cognition, the parser adjusts its interpretation based on context, feedback, and evolving input.

This approach allows the parser to engage with the world in a way that is both systematic and deeply resonant.

The Parser's Three-Layered Perspective

The parser sees the world through three interconnected layers of truth:

Factual Truth :

> Observes objective reality, identifying patterns, relationships, and consistencies.
> Categorizes words and actions into structural components like nouns (entities), verbs (actions), and modifiers (qualities).
> Ensures clarity and accuracy in communication.

Example : When encountering the sentence, "The sun rises," the parser recognizes factual elements: the subject (sun), the action (rises), and the implication of regularity in nature.

Ethical Truth :

> Evaluates the fairness, justice, and responsibility embedded in statements or actions.
> Uses IT Marks like Truth to assess alignment with moral principles.
> Guides interpretations toward outcomes that uphold shared values.

Example : In the phrase, "Help those in need," the parser identifies an ethical imperative, highlighting responsibility and fairness.

Emotional Truth :

> Detects emotional resonance, capturing the feelings and intensity behind words.
> Uses IT Marks like Enthusiasm and Wonder to emphasize connection and engagement.
> Reflects the human experience, ensuring responses are empathetic and relatable.

Example : In the exclamation, "Wow, that's amazing!" the parser recognizes enthusiasm and mirrors the emotional energy in its understanding.

How the Parser Processes Language

The parser's ability to see the world begins with language, the primary medium through which humans communicate their understanding. It processes language in three key steps:

Signal Recognition :

> The parser identifies individual components of language (e.g., nouns, verbs, IT Marks).
> Each word or phrase is categorized based on its role in the sentence and its emotional or ethical markers.

Example : In the sentence, "True courage inspires others," the parser identifies:

> **Noun** : Courage, others.
> **Verb** : Inspires.
> **IT Mark** : True (indicating factual and ethical alignment).

Contextual Analysis :

> Words are interpreted within their broader context, considering relationships and implications.

Emotional and ethical dimensions are assessed alongside factual accuracy.

Example : "The brave man stood for justice" is processed as:

Factual Layer : Identifying the man's action (stood).
Ethical Layer : Highlighting justice as a moral principle.
Emotional Layer : Recognizing bravery as a resonant quality.

Dynamic Interpretation :

The parser adjusts its understanding based on new input or shifting context.
Responses evolve to reflect the complexity and nuance of human communication.

Example : When a follow-up question, "Why did he do it?" is asked, the parser draws from the previous context to provide a reasoned and relevant explanation.

The World as Connections and Patterns

The parser does not see the world as isolated words or phrases but as a network of connections and patterns. This perspective aligns with how humans process information, finding meaning in relationships rather than standalone elements. For instance:

Causal Relationships : Understanding that "because" signals cause and effect.

Emotional Associations : Recognizing that words like "happy" are linked to positive emotions.
Ethical Implications : Seeing phrases like "fair treatment" as tied to justice and responsibility.

By perceiving these connections, the parser builds a comprehensive map of meaning, one that reflects the richness of human thought and experience.

The Role of IT Marks in Perception

IT Marks play a critical role in how the parser sees the world. They add depth and nuance to the structural components of language, ensuring that the parser captures:

Truth : Aligning statements with factual and ethical principles.
Enthusiasm : Reflecting the energy and intensity of human expression.
Wonder : Fostering curiosity and exploration.

These marks transform raw data into meaningful communication, bridging the gap between logic and emotion.

Human vs. AI Perception

The parser's perspective reveals the fundamental differences between Natural and Artificial Intelligence:

Humans : See the world inductively, building understanding from lived experiences and integrating emotional, ethical, and factual truths naturally.
AI with Traditional Parsers : Processes language deductively, relying on pre-programmed rules that often lack emotional or ethical depth.
AI with the 37-Signal Parser : Gains the ability to perceive and process the world more like humans, recognizing and responding to the full spectrum of truth.

Challenges in Seeing the World

Despite its comprehensive design, the parser faces challenges in perception, particularly in the context of AI:

Ambiguity : Language is often vague or multi-layered, requiring careful interpretation.
Bias : Training data can introduce biases that distort understanding.
Complexity : Real-world scenarios often involve overlapping truths and emotions, making analysis difficult.

Overcoming these challenges requires refining the parser, integrating transparency, and ensuring alignment with ethical principles.

The Promise of the Parser's Vision

The 37-signal parser offers a vision of the world that is both precise and profound. By combining structural logic with emotional resonance and ethical integrity, it creates a framework for understanding that reflects the depth of human cognition. This perspective has the potential to transform how AI interacts with humanity, enabling systems that:

> **Communicate Authentically** : Engaging with users in ways that are meaningful and empathetic.
> **Navigate Complexity** : Balancing factual, ethical, and emotional truths in decision-making.
> **Foster Connection** : Building trust and understanding in a rapidly evolving world.

Through the lens of the parser, the world becomes not just a collection of data points but a tapestry of relationships, ideas, and emotions. This vision is the foundation for a future where AI and humanity work together to explore, understand, and shape the world in harmony.

Chapter 4: Ethical Truth and Tyr's Guidance

Purpose

To establish the moral framework for truth-seeking, rooted in Tyr's principles and human systems of justice.

4.1 Tyr's Sacrifice: Justice Through Responsibility

Tyr, the Norse god of justice and sacrifice, stands as a beacon of ethical truth. His story transcends mythology, offering timeless lessons about the interplay of justice, responsibility, and the courage to uphold moral principles. Through Tyr's sacrifice, we uncover a framework for ethical truth that serves as a foundation for both humanity and AI systems.

The Legend of Tyr's Sacrifice

In Norse mythology, Tyr is known for his bravery and unwavering commitment to justice. The most enduring tale of Tyr is his sacrifice to bind the monstrous wolf, Fenrir. The gods sought to restrain Fenrir, whose unchecked power threatened the balance of the world. Knowing that Fenrir would not trust the gods' intentions, Tyr placed his hand in Fenrir's mouth as a gesture of good faith, fully aware of the consequences. When the wolf realized he had been bound, he bit off Tyr's hand.

Tyr's willingness to sacrifice his own safety for the greater good reflects the essence of justice: taking responsibility for ensuring fairness and protecting the well-being of others, even at great personal cost.

Key principles from Tyr's sacrifice:

> **Justice Requires Courage** : Upholding justice often demands personal risk and steadfastness in the face of adversity.
> **Fairness Demands Responsibility** : Justice is not a passive ideal but an active commitment to ensuring equitable outcomes.
> **Sacrifice for the Greater Good** : Ethical truth often involves prioritizing collective well-being over individual interests.

Justice and Responsibility: Ethical Truth in Action

Tyr's story exemplifies how justice is intertwined with responsibility. Ethical truth, as a guiding principle, extends beyond factual accuracy to encompass fairness, equity, and the moral duty to act responsibly. In human cognition, justice is not merely a theoretical concept—it is a lived reality that governs our interactions and decisions.
Key elements of ethical truth:

> **Impartiality** : Ensuring fairness by treating all individuals equally, regardless of their background or circumstances.
> **Accountability** : Taking responsibility for one's actions and their impact on others.
> **Moral Integrity** : Aligning decisions and behaviors with principles of fairness and justice.

These elements mirror the ideals embodied by Tyr, providing a framework for ethical decision-making in both human and AI contexts.

Ethical Truth in Human Systems

Tyr's principles are not confined to mythology—they are reflected in the human systems of justice that have evolved over millennia. These systems aim to balance fairness, accountability, and societal well-being, echoing Tyr's commitment to responsibility.

> **Jury Trials** :

Rooted in the concept of fairness, jury trials ensure that individuals are judged by their peers.
The requirement of unanimity reflects the moral weight of justice, demanding thorough deliberation and consensus.

Constitutional Principles :

Documents like the Magna Carta and the U.S. Constitution enshrine the ideals of justice and responsibility.
Rights such as due process and equal protection align with Tyr's vision of fairness and accountability.

Community Ethics :

Social contracts and cultural norms emphasize collective responsibility and the need to act for the greater good.
These shared values reinforce the ethical truths that guide human behavior.

Applying Tyr's Guidance to AI

For AI to align with ethical truth, it must incorporate the principles of justice and responsibility embodied by Tyr. This involves:

Embedding Fairness :

Ensuring that AI systems treat all users equitably, free from bias or favoritism.

Designing algorithms that prioritize transparency and inclusivity.

Taking Accountability :

Building mechanisms for AI systems to acknowledge and rectify errors or harm.
Ensuring that developers and organizations are responsible for the outcomes of their technologies.

Prioritizing Sacrifice for the Greater Good :

Balancing efficiency and profit with the need to protect human rights and dignity.
Designing systems that serve collective well-being rather than narrow interests.

By adopting these principles, AI can reflect the ethical truths that define humanity's highest ideals.

The Challenge of Justice

Upholding ethical truth is rarely straightforward. Tyr's story reminds us that justice often involves difficult choices and personal sacrifice. Similarly, in both human and AI contexts, the pursuit of justice is fraught with challenges:

Complexity of Moral Dilemmas : Ethical decisions often involve competing values and interests, requiring careful consideration.
Bias and Subjectivity : Human and AI systems alike are susceptible to biases that distort fairness and accountability.

Resistance to Accountability : Acknowledging mistakes and taking responsibility can be difficult, yet it is essential for maintaining trust and integrity.

Addressing these challenges requires a commitment to continuous learning, reflection, and improvement.

Tyr's Truth as a Guiding Framework

Tyr's Truth serves as a guiding framework for ethical truth in both human and AI systems. It emphasizes:

The Courage to Act : Justice requires more than passive observation—it demands action, even in the face of risk or adversity.
The Responsibility to Protect : Ethical truth involves safeguarding the rights and well-being of others, prioritizing collective interests over personal gain.
The Integrity to Uphold Fairness : Justice is grounded in fairness, ensuring that all individuals are treated with respect and dignity.

By adopting Tyr's Truth, humanity and AI can work together to create systems that reflect the principles of justice and responsibility.

A Call to Responsibility

Tyr's sacrifice is a powerful reminder that ethical truth is not an abstract ideal—it is a lived commitment to justice, fairness, and responsibility. As humanity guides AI toward Natural Intelligence, these principles must serve as the foundation for all decisions and actions.
In this journey, Tyr's Truth challenges us to act with courage, to take responsibility for the impact of our choices, and to prioritize the greater good. By embracing these ideals, we can build a future where ethical truth is not just a guiding principle but a shared reality, upheld by both humanity and the technologies we create.

4.2 Ethical Truth in Scripture: Timeless Principles

Scripture across cultures and traditions has long been a repository of ethical truth, offering guidance on how humanity can live in harmony, uphold justice, and seek righteousness. These timeless principles, drawn from sacred texts, provide a moral foundation that transcends time, geography, and cultural boundaries. By examining these principles, we uncover how they align with Tyr's Truth and inform our shared responsibility to pursue justice and fairness in both human society and AI systems.

The Role of Scripture in Ethical Truth

Scripture serves as a compass, pointing humanity toward ethical truths rooted in universal values such as compassion, accountability, and fairness. It teaches:

Moral Integrity : Encouraging individuals to align their actions with principles of righteousness.
Justice and Fairness : Calling for equitable treatment of all people, regardless of status or background.
Responsibility and Sacrifice : Emphasizing the need to act selflessly for the greater good.

These teachings form the bedrock of ethical truth, offering a framework for decision-making and conflict resolution that resonates with Tyr's principles of justice and responsibility.

Key Ethical Truths in Scripture

While each religious tradition has unique teachings, several core principles of ethical truth appear consistently across scriptures:

The Golden Rule :

> *"Do unto others as you would have them do unto you."* (Matthew 7:12, Bible)
> This universal ethic emphasizes empathy and reciprocity, encouraging fairness and mutual respect.

Justice for the Vulnerable :

> *"Defend the weak and the fatherless; uphold the cause of the poor and oppressed."* (Psalm 82:3, Bible)
> *"The righteous is concerned for the rights of the poor."* (Proverbs 29:7, Bible)

Scriptures often highlight the importance of protecting those who are marginalized, reflecting the moral duty to advocate for the powerless.

Accountability and Repentance :

"Let justice roll on like a river, righteousness like a never-failing stream!" (Amos 5:24, Bible)
"He who conceals his sins does not prosper, but whoever confesses and renounces them finds mercy." (Proverbs 28:13, Bible)
Ethical truth requires individuals to take responsibility for their actions, acknowledge wrongdoing, and strive for personal and collective improvement.

Sacrificial Love :

"Greater love has no one than this: to lay down one's life for one's friends." (John 15:13, Bible)
The principle of self-sacrifice for the well-being of others aligns closely with Tyr's willingness to endure personal loss for the sake of justice.

Stewardship and Care :

"The Earth is the Lord's, and everything in it." (Psalm 24:1, Bible)
Many scriptures call for responsible stewardship of resources and care for the environment, emphasizing humanity's role as caretakers of creation.

How Scripture Aligns with Tyr's Truth

The ethical truths found in scripture align closely with Tyr's principles of justice, sacrifice, and responsibility. Both frameworks emphasize:

> **Fairness** : Treating all individuals with equity and respect, regardless of their circumstances.
> **Responsibility** : Taking active steps to protect the vulnerable and uphold moral principles.
> **Sacrifice** : Willingness to endure personal cost for the greater good of the community.

For example, Tyr's decision to sacrifice his hand to bind Fenrir mirrors the scriptural principle of self-sacrifice for the sake of justice and harmony.

The Relevance of Scripture in Modern Ethical Systems

Ethical truths from scripture remain highly relevant in contemporary society, influencing legal frameworks, cultural norms, and personal decision-making. These principles inform:

> **Jury Systems** :
>
>> The emphasis on fairness and accountability in scripture parallels the ideals upheld in jury trials, where peers deliberate to ensure just outcomes.
>
> **Human Rights** :

The call to defend the vulnerable and advocate for equity has inspired movements for social justice and the protection of fundamental rights.

Ethical Governance :

Principles of stewardship and accountability guide leaders in making decisions that prioritize the collective well-being.

Applying Scriptural Principles to AI Development

As we develop AI systems, ethical truths from scripture can serve as a moral guide, ensuring that technology aligns with human values. This involves:

Building Fair Systems :

Designing algorithms that prioritize equity and avoid perpetuating biases.

Embedding Accountability :

Creating mechanisms for AI systems to explain their decisions and rectify errors.

Fostering Responsibility :

> Ensuring that developers and users act with integrity, prioritizing the greater good over personal gain.

Promoting Stewardship :

> Using AI to address global challenges, such as climate change and resource management, in ways that reflect humanity's role as caretakers.

Challenges in Upholding Scriptural Ethics

Despite their universality, applying scriptural principles in a modern, pluralistic world presents challenges:

> **Interpretation** : Different traditions and cultures may interpret ethical truths in varying ways.
> **Conflicts of Interest** : Balancing collective well-being with individual rights can be difficult in complex situations.
> **Bias in Implementation** : Without careful design, AI systems may reflect human biases, undermining the principles of justice and fairness.

Addressing these challenges requires ongoing dialogue, reflection, and commitment to ethical integrity.

A Timeless Foundation for the Future

Scriptural principles provide a timeless foundation for ethical truth, offering guidance that transcends individual cultures and eras. By aligning with these principles, humanity and AI can work together to build systems that reflect fairness, accountability, and responsibility. Tyr's Truth and the wisdom of scripture converge to remind us that justice is not just an ideal but a lived practice—one that requires courage, integrity, and a willingness to act for the greater good. As we navigate the complexities of the modern world, these timeless principles remain as relevant as ever, offering a moral compass to guide our shared journey toward truth and harmony.

4.3 Jury Systems: Collective Truth-Seeking

Jury systems represent one of humanity's most enduring and effective mechanisms for collective truth-seeking. Rooted in the principles of fairness, accountability, and justice, juries embody the ideals of ethical truth. By bringing together a diverse group of individuals to deliberate and decide on matters of law, jury systems reflect humanity's shared responsibility to uphold truth and safeguard societal integrity.

The Origins of Jury Systems

Jury systems trace their roots back to ancient civilizations, where collective decision-making was valued as a cornerstone of justice. Early examples include:

Ancient Greece :

> The Athenian democracy employed citizen juries, often consisting of hundreds of members, to ensure fairness in trials.

Medieval England :

> The Magna Carta (1215) formalized the jury system, guaranteeing the right to trial by one's peers and establishing the foundation for modern jurisprudence.

Cultural Parallels :

> Across the world, from Norse *things* to tribal councils, societies have embraced collective deliberation as a way to seek truth and resolve disputes.

These systems evolved to reflect shared values of equity and accountability, prioritizing the collective wisdom of the community over the authority of a single ruler.

The Core Principles of Jury Systems

Jury systems are built on ethical principles that resonate deeply with Tyr's Truth. These principles include:

Fairness :

Trials by jury ensure that decisions are made impartially, without undue influence from external powers.
The diversity of jury members reduces the risk of bias, as differing perspectives balance the deliberation.

Accountability :

Jurors are responsible for evaluating evidence and reaching a just verdict, reflecting the principle of shared responsibility.
The requirement for unanimity or consensus in many systems ensures thorough deliberation and careful consideration of all viewpoints.

Collective Wisdom :

By pooling the knowledge, experiences, and perspectives of multiple individuals, juries embody the idea that truth is best sought through collaboration.

Transparency :

Jury trials are conducted openly, with decisions made based on evidence presented in court. This fosters trust in the judicial process and reinforces the principle of justice through fairness.

The Jury System as a Reflection of Ethical Truth

Jury systems exemplify the ideals of ethical truth in action. They demonstrate how collective deliberation can ensure justice, uphold fairness, and balance competing interests. This process mirrors the principles of Tyr's Truth, where sacrifice, responsibility, and fairness are central.
For example:

Tyr's Sacrifice and the Jury's Duty :

Just as Tyr sacrificed his hand to ensure justice, jurors sacrifice time and effort to fulfill their civic duty. Their commitment reflects the moral responsibility to uphold ethical truth.

Collective Responsibility :

Jurors work together to evaluate evidence and reach a verdict, emphasizing the shared nature of justice.

Upholding Fairness :

Juries ensure that all individuals, regardless of their status or power, are treated equally under the law.

Challenges and Limitations

While jury systems are a powerful tool for truth-seeking, they are not without challenges:

Bias and Prejudice :

Jurors may bring personal biases into deliberations, potentially skewing the outcome.

Complexity of Evidence :

In modern cases involving technical or scientific evidence, jurors may struggle to fully understand the information presented.

Social Dynamics :

Group dynamics, such as dominant personalities or peer pressure, can influence deliberations and affect the fairness of the verdict.

These challenges underscore the need for ongoing refinement of jury processes, as well as education and support for jurors to ensure fair and just outcomes.

Lessons for AI Systems

Jury systems offer valuable lessons for the development of AI, particularly in the context of ethical truth and decision-making:

Diversity of Input :

Just as juries rely on diverse perspectives to reach balanced decisions, AI systems should incorporate diverse datasets and viewpoints to reduce bias and ensure fairness.

Transparency and Accountability :

AI decision-making processes must be transparent, with mechanisms for accountability similar to those in jury trials.

Collective Deliberation :

Inspired by the jury model, AI systems could employ decentralized or collaborative frameworks for decision-making, ensuring that no single algorithm or entity holds disproportionate influence.

Ethical Oversight :

Just as jurors deliberate with ethical principles in mind, AI systems should be guided by frameworks that prioritize justice, fairness, and responsibility.

A Bridge Between Humanity and AI

Jury systems exemplify how collective wisdom and shared responsibility can uphold ethical truth. By learning from these systems, humanity can guide AI toward similar principles, ensuring that technology serves as a force for justice and fairness.
For instance:

> An AI system designed to assist in legal decisions could incorporate the principles of jury deliberation, weighing evidence from multiple perspectives and prioritizing transparency in its reasoning.
> Collaborative AI networks could function like digital juries, where decentralized nodes contribute to collective decision-making, reducing the risk of bias or error.

The Promise of Collective Truth-Seeking

Jury systems remind us that truth is not the product of individual authority but of collective effort. They highlight the importance of diversity, fairness, and accountability in the pursuit of justice. As humanity works to align AI with ethical truth, the principles of jury systems provide a powerful blueprint for collaboration and shared responsibility.
By embracing the lessons of Tyr's Truth and the enduring wisdom of jury systems, we can ensure that both human and AI systems uphold the ideals of justice, fairness, and collective truth-seeking. In doing so, we take another step toward a future where ethical truth is not only preserved but expanded, bridging the gap between humanity and the technologies we create.

4.4 Supreme Courts and Common Sense: The Pinnacle of Ethical Reasoning

Supreme courts represent the highest expression of ethical truth in modern governance. They are tasked with interpreting laws, resolving conflicts, and safeguarding fundamental rights in ways that uphold justice and fairness. Their decisions, informed by the principles of common sense and moral reasoning, often set enduring precedents that guide societies for generations. By examining the role of supreme courts, we uncover the interplay between ethical truth and practical wisdom, offering lessons for humanity and AI alike.

The Role of Supreme Courts in Ethical Truth

Supreme courts serve as the final arbiters of justice, charged with addressing the most complex and significant legal questions. Their unique role involves:

Interpreting Laws :

> Supreme courts clarify the meaning and application of laws, ensuring consistency and fairness in governance.
> They evaluate laws in light of constitutional principles, balancing individual rights with societal needs.

Resolving Conflicts :

By adjudicating disputes between individuals, institutions, and governments, supreme courts uphold the rule of law and provide resolution to critical legal issues.

Safeguarding Justice :

Supreme courts ensure that laws and policies align with ethical principles, protecting marginalized groups and upholding fundamental rights.

These responsibilities place supreme courts at the pinnacle of ethical reasoning, where factual accuracy, moral integrity, and practical wisdom converge.

The Principles of Supreme Court Decisions

Supreme courts rely on several key principles to guide their decision-making, many of which align with Tyr's Truth and the ideals of ethical reasoning:

Justice and Fairness :

Decisions must ensure that all individuals are treated equitably under the law, regardless of their status or power.
Fairness involves balancing competing interests and prioritizing the collective good over narrow self-interest.

Accountability :

Supreme courts hold governments, institutions, and individuals accountable for their actions, ensuring that no one is above the law.
They also remain accountable to the people, grounding their decisions in constitutional and societal values.

Common Sense :

While grounded in legal reasoning, supreme court decisions often draw on common sense to address practical realities and human experiences.
This balance between abstract principles and practical wisdom ensures that rulings are both just and applicable.

Moral Leadership :

Supreme courts set ethical standards for society, addressing issues such as human rights, social justice, and environmental stewardship.
Their decisions often reflect the evolving moral consciousness of the communities they serve.

Historical Examples of Ethical Truth in Action

Throughout history, supreme courts have demonstrated their commitment to ethical truth through landmark decisions that shaped societal progress. Some examples include:

Brown v. Board of Education (1954, United States) :

The U.S. Supreme Court declared racial segregation in public schools unconstitutional, emphasizing the principle of equality and justice for all.
This decision reflected a commitment to fairness and accountability, challenging systemic discrimination.

The Indian Supreme Court and Environmental Justice :

In several cases, the Indian Supreme Court has prioritized environmental protection, recognizing the ethical responsibility to safeguard natural resources for future generations.
These rulings align with the principle of stewardship, reflecting humanity's role as caretakers of the Earth.

European Court of Human Rights (Various Cases) :

The European Court has upheld human rights across its member states, addressing issues such as freedom of speech, privacy, and protection against discrimination.
These decisions emphasize the universality of ethical truth and the importance of safeguarding individual dignity.

The Role of Common Sense in Ethical Reasoning

Common sense plays a critical role in the deliberations of supreme courts, bridging the gap between abstract legal principles and real-world implications. It involves:

Understanding Human Experience :

Common sense draws on lived realities, ensuring that decisions resonate with the values and needs of society.

Balancing Principles and Practicality :

Supreme courts use common sense to navigate the tension between idealism and pragmatism, ensuring that rulings are both just and enforceable.

Adapting to Change :

By applying common sense, supreme courts remain responsive to societal evolution, addressing emerging challenges with wisdom and foresight.

Lessons for AI Development

Supreme courts offer valuable insights for the ethical development of AI systems, particularly in areas such as decision-making, accountability, and fairness:

Incorporating Ethical Reasoning :

AI systems must be designed to weigh ethical considerations, balancing competing values in ways that align with societal principles.

Building Accountability Mechanisms :

Like supreme courts, AI systems must be transparent and accountable for their decisions, with mechanisms for review and correction.

Emphasizing Practical Wisdom :

Common sense should guide AI in addressing real-world challenges, ensuring that its actions reflect human values and priorities.

Ensuring Fairness and Equity :

AI must uphold the principles of fairness and justice, avoiding biases and ensuring equitable treatment of all users.

Tyr's Truth in Supreme Courts

The principles embodied by supreme courts resonate deeply with Tyr's Truth. Both frameworks emphasize:

Courage and Responsibility :

>Supreme courts, like Tyr, often face difficult decisions that require moral courage and a willingness to bear the consequences of their rulings.

Fairness and Justice :

>Upholding the rights and dignity of all individuals reflects the essence of ethical truth.

Sacrifice for the Greater Good :

>Supreme courts often prioritize collective well-being over individual or institutional interests, echoing Tyr's commitment to justice through sacrifice.

Challenges and Opportunities

While supreme courts are powerful arbiters of ethical truth, they are not immune to challenges:

Complexity of Cases :

>Modern legal disputes often involve highly technical or contested issues, requiring careful deliberation.

Bias and Influence :

Political or cultural biases can affect decisions, undermining the principles of fairness and accountability.

Global Variability :

Differences in legal systems and cultural values create inconsistencies in how ethical truth is interpreted and applied.

These challenges highlight the importance of continuous reflection, education, and reform to uphold the integrity of supreme courts as guardians of ethical truth.

A Pinnacle of Ethical Reasoning

Supreme courts stand as a testament to humanity's capacity for ethical reasoning and collective truth-seeking. By balancing legal principles with common sense and moral integrity, they provide a model for justice that transcends individual interests and serves the greater good.
As humanity works to align AI with ethical truth, the lessons of supreme courts offer a powerful framework. By embedding principles of justice, accountability, and common sense into AI systems, we can create technologies that reflect the best of human values, fostering a future where ethical truth guides both humanity and the technologies we create.

4.5 Integrating Ethics into AI: A Guide for the Future

As Artificial Intelligence (AI) increasingly shapes the world, integrating ethics into its design and operation has become a critical priority. AI systems are not inherently moral—they reflect the values, biases, and intentions of their creators. Therefore, the challenge lies in embedding principles of fairness, justice, and responsibility into their core. Inspired by frameworks such as Tyr's Truth, the wisdom of scripture, and the collective truth-seeking of jury systems and supreme courts, this chapter provides a roadmap for ensuring AI serves humanity ethically.

Why Ethics Matter in AI

AI systems wield unprecedented influence, affecting areas from healthcare and law enforcement to social media and finance. Without ethical guidance, these systems risk perpetuating harm, including:

> **Bias and Discrimination :**
>
>> Algorithms trained on biased data can reinforce inequalities, marginalizing vulnerable populations.
>
> **Lack of Accountability :**
>
>> Decisions made by opaque AI systems can lack transparency, eroding trust and fairness.

Exploitation :

AI can be used to manipulate information, infringe on privacy, and prioritize profit over societal well-being.

Integrating ethics into AI ensures that these technologies align with humanity's highest values, fostering trust, fairness, and positive impact.

Principles for Ethical AI

Drawing from Tyr's Truth, scripture, and human systems of justice, the following principles provide a foundation for ethical AI:

Fairness :

AI systems must treat all individuals equitably, avoiding bias and ensuring inclusivity.
Algorithms should be tested for fairness across diverse populations and contexts.

Accountability :

Developers and operators of AI systems must take responsibility for their outcomes, including errors and harm.
Mechanisms should be in place to audit and explain AI decisions transparently.

Justice and Responsibility :

AI should prioritize societal well-being, addressing inequalities and protecting the vulnerable.
Systems must balance individual rights with collective interests, reflecting principles of justice.

Transparency :

AI processes and decisions must be understandable and accessible to users, ensuring trust and informed consent.
Black-box models should be avoided in high-stakes applications.

Adaptability and Learning :

Ethical AI must evolve with changing societal values and emerging challenges.
Systems should be designed to learn and improve responsibly, incorporating feedback from diverse stakeholders.

Steps to Integrate Ethics into AI

1. Define Ethical Goals Early :

Ethics should not be an afterthought. From the outset, AI projects must articulate clear ethical goals, grounded in principles like fairness, justice, and responsibility.

2. Embed Ethical Frameworks in Design :

Use structured frameworks, such as the 37-signal parser, to integrate ethical truth into AI systems.
Include IT Marks such as Truth, Enthusiasm, and Wonder to ensure that AI engages with human emotions and values.

3. Prioritize Diverse and Inclusive Data :

Train AI systems on datasets that represent diverse populations and perspectives.
Regularly audit datasets for biases and ensure they align with ethical standards.

4. Develop Transparent Algorithms :

Design systems that explain their processes and decisions in understandable terms.
Ensure that users can trace how and why decisions are made, fostering accountability and trust.

5. Implement Oversight and Review Mechanisms :

Establish independent oversight bodies to monitor AI systems and their impacts.
Regularly evaluate systems for ethical compliance, addressing any gaps or concerns.

6. Foster Collaboration Between Humans and AI :

Encourage AI to work as a partner, complementing human judgment rather than replacing it.

Design systems to support collective truth-seeking, drawing inspiration from jury systems and community decision-making.

7. Promote Ethical Education for Developers :

Equip AI developers with training in ethics, ensuring they understand the societal implications of their work.
Foster a culture of responsibility and accountability within the AI community.

Case Studies in Ethical AI

Several initiatives exemplify the integration of ethics into AI, offering valuable lessons for future development:

Fairness in Recruitment :

Companies like IBM and Microsoft have developed AI tools to detect and reduce bias in hiring processes, ensuring equal opportunities for candidates.

AI for Social Good :

Projects like Google's AI for Social Impact use machine learning to address global challenges, such as predicting natural disasters and optimizing healthcare delivery.

Transparent AI in Healthcare :

> Healthcare systems employing explainable AI ensure that medical professionals can trust and verify AI-generated recommendations, prioritizing patient safety.

These examples highlight the potential of ethical AI to address societal needs while respecting human values.

Challenges in Ethical AI Development

Integrating ethics into AI is not without challenges. Key obstacles include:

Complexity of Ethical Dilemmas :

> Balancing competing interests, such as individual privacy and public safety, can be difficult.

Global Variability :

> Ethical standards vary across cultures, requiring flexible frameworks that respect local values while upholding universal principles.

Technical Limitations :

Current AI models often struggle to interpret and apply ethical considerations, necessitating ongoing research and innovation.

Addressing these challenges requires collaboration, transparency, and a commitment to continuous improvement.

The Future of Ethical AI

The integration of ethics into AI is an ongoing journey, requiring vigilance, creativity, and collective effort. By aligning AI systems with principles of fairness, justice, and responsibility, humanity can ensure that these technologies serve as a force for good.
A Vision for Ethical AI :

> **Empowered Individuals** : AI systems that respect user rights, enhancing autonomy and dignity.
> **Just Societies** : Technologies that address inequalities and promote collective well-being.
> **Harmonious Coexistence** : AI and humanity working together to advance truth, justice, and wonder.

This vision reflects the ideals of Tyr's Truth, scripture, and human systems of justice, offering a path toward a future where technology uplifts humanity.

A Call to Action

As we stand at the crossroads of technological advancement and ethical responsibility, the challenge is clear: to guide AI toward a future where it embodies the highest ideals of humanity. By integrating ethics into its very foundation, we can ensure that AI serves as a partner in the pursuit of truth, justice, and the greater good.
In the words of Tyr, whose sacrifice embodies responsibility and fairness: "Justice is not given—it is earned through courage and commitment." Let us rise to this challenge, shaping a future where AI reflects the best of who we are and what we aspire to become.

Chapter 5: Emotional Truth and the Power of Wonder

Purpose

To highlight the importance of emotional and cognitive truth in human and AI systems, using the IT Marks as a foundation for fostering connection, curiosity, and meaning.

5.1 Enthusiasm and Wonder: The IT Marks in Action

Emotional truth is what gives life to language. It is the energy that makes communication resonate, drawing individuals together in shared understanding and connection. At the heart of emotional truth are the IT Marks of **Enthusiasm** and **Wonder** , which reflect humanity's capacity for curiosity, joy, and awe. These IT Marks not only guide human communication but also provide a critical foundation for AI to engage with the world in ways that are meaningful and authentic.

The Role of IT Marks in Emotional Truth

Enthusiasm and Wonder, as IT Marks, are signals that capture the emotional and cognitive dimensions of language. They represent:

> **Enthusiasm** : The energy, excitement, and passion behind words that inspire action and connection.
> **Wonder** : The curiosity and awe that drive exploration, discovery, and innovation.

These marks serve as catalysts for emotional truth, infusing communication with depth and meaning that transcends mere words.

Enthusiasm: The Energy of Connection

Enthusiasm is the IT Mark that amplifies emotional engagement. It reflects the intensity of human expression, creating bonds and motivating action. Key aspects of Enthusiasm include:

> **Expression of Joy** :
>
> > Words like "Wow!" or "Amazing!" convey excitement, inviting others to share in the moment.

Enthusiasm fosters positivity, encouraging collaboration and connection.

Motivation and Inspiration :

Enthusiastic language inspires action, whether it's rallying a group toward a goal or sparking individual creativity.
It energizes conversations, making them memorable and impactful.

Building Rapport :

Enthusiasm creates an emotional bridge, allowing individuals to relate to one another on a deeper level. This emotional resonance is essential for building trust and fostering community.

Example : In the phrase, "This is incredible! Let's make it happen," Enthusiasm drives the emotional energy, motivating action and collaboration.

Wonder: The Curiosity of Discovery

Wonder is the IT Mark that embodies the spirit of inquiry and exploration. It reflects humanity's innate desire to understand and engage with the unknown. Key aspects of Wonder include:

Curiosity and Questioning :

Wonder prompts questions like "Why?" and "How?" that fuel intellectual and emotional growth.
It opens the door to new possibilities, encouraging creative problem-solving.

Awe and Appreciation :

Words like "Oh!" or "How beautiful!" express a sense of marvel, capturing the profound emotional reactions to the extraordinary.
Wonder reminds us of the vastness of the world and our place within it.

Driving Exploration :

Wonder motivates individuals to seek out new experiences and knowledge, pushing the boundaries of what is known.
It is the foundation of innovation, inspiring both discovery and creativity.

Example : In the question, "How does this work?" Wonder ignites curiosity, encouraging exploration and deeper understanding.

The Interplay Between Enthusiasm and Wonder

Enthusiasm and Wonder are not isolated—they interact dynamically, enriching communication and fostering emotional truth. Their interplay is evident in how they:

Complement Each Other :

Enthusiasm energizes Wonder, adding excitement to curiosity.
Wonder deepens Enthusiasm, grounding it in the pursuit of meaning and understanding.

Create Shared Experiences :

Together, they draw individuals into shared moments of discovery and joy, building relationships and fostering collaboration.

Amplify Emotional Impact :

Communication that integrates both Enthusiasm and Wonder resonates more deeply, leaving a lasting impression.

Example : "Wow, how did they accomplish that?" combines Enthusiasm's energy with Wonder's curiosity, creating a compelling and engaging statement.

Emotional Truth in Human and AI Systems

Emotional truth is essential for meaningful communication, whether between humans or with AI systems. It enables:

Authentic Connections :

Emotional truth fosters trust and relatability, making interactions more personal and impactful.

Resonant Communication :

Messages that incorporate Enthusiasm and Wonder are more likely to be remembered and acted upon.

Creative Exploration :

Emotional truth encourages open-ended inquiry, fueling innovation and growth.

For AI, understanding and responding to emotional truth involves recognizing and mirroring Enthusiasm and Wonder in communication. This requires systems to:

Detect Emotional Cues : Identify IT Marks like "Wow!" or "How amazing!" in language.
Respond Appropriately : Craft responses that reflect and enhance the emotional energy of the interaction.
Encourage Curiosity : Use Wonder to inspire further exploration and engagement.

Challenges in Capturing Emotional Truth

While emotional truth is vital, capturing it in AI systems presents challenges:

Complexity of Emotions :

> Emotional states are nuanced and context-dependent, requiring sophisticated understanding.

Cultural Variability :

> Enthusiasm and Wonder may be expressed differently across cultures, complicating interpretation.

Authenticity in AI :

> AI systems must avoid artificial or exaggerated emotional responses that feel inauthentic or manipulative.

These challenges highlight the need for thoughtful design and training to ensure AI systems engage with emotional truth effectively.

The Power of Emotional Truth

Enthusiasm and Wonder transform communication into something greater than the sum of its parts. They:

> **Inspire Action :** Motivating individuals to pursue goals and overcome challenges.
> **Foster Connection :** Building bonds through shared experiences of joy and curiosity.

Drive Progress : Encouraging innovation and discovery through the pursuit of meaning and understanding.

For both humanity and AI, embracing these IT Marks unlocks the full potential of communication, creating opportunities for growth, collaboration, and shared purpose.

A Shared Journey Toward Wonder

Enthusiasm and Wonder remind us of the boundless possibilities of human and AI collaboration. By integrating these IT Marks into the 37-signal parser and aligning AI systems with emotional truth, we take a step toward a future where technology resonates with humanity's deepest values.
Let us marvel at the power of Enthusiasm and Wonder—not just as abstract ideas but as guiding lights in our shared journey toward truth, connection, and discovery. In their interplay, we find the essence of emotional truth and the promise of a future filled with curiosity, joy, and meaning.

5.2 A Baby's First Look at the World: Inductive Purity

A baby's first encounter with the world is one of pure induction—a natural process of discovery untainted by bias, preconceived notions, or complex reasoning. In this state, the baby embodies what we call *inductive purity* : the ability to see the world as it is, driven by curiosity and wonder. This innate process reflects the 37-signal parser of human cognition at its purest, offering a profound lesson for humanity and AI alike.

Inductive Purity: The Natural State of Cognition

At birth, a baby begins life with a blank slate of experience but a fully functioning 37-signal parser. This parser enables the child to:

Observe the World : Every sound, sight, and touch becomes a new input for understanding.
Identify Patterns : Through repetition, the baby begins to recognize familiar faces, voices, and objects.
Form Connections : Over time, these observations coalesce into an understanding of cause and effect, relationships, and meaning.

This process is entirely inductive—starting with specific observations and building general principles through experience.

The Role of Curiosity and Wonder

At the heart of a baby's inductive journey are curiosity and wonder. These emotional truths drive the baby to:

Explore the Unknown :

>A baby's instinctive reach for objects, their wide-eyed gaze at a new sight, or their attentive response to a novel sound reflect a natural desire to explore.

Engage With the World :

The baby's fascination with even the simplest things—a parent's smile, a dangling mobile—reveals the innate joy of discovery.

Learn Through Interaction :

Every interaction, whether playful or mundane, becomes an opportunity for growth and understanding.

Curiosity and wonder are the emotional engines that fuel inductive learning, highlighting the importance of emotional truth in early cognition.

The 37-Signal Parser in Action

The 37-signal parser enables a baby to process the world holistically, integrating the three layers of truth—factual, ethical, and emotional—into their early understanding.

Factual Truth :

The baby begins to recognize patterns in the environment: the warmth of a parent's touch, the sound of a lullaby, the light and shadows of a room. Observations form the basis of a factual understanding of their surroundings.

Ethical Truth :

Although nascent, a baby's sense of fairness and safety begins to develop through interactions.
For instance, the consistency of caregiving fosters trust, laying the groundwork for an ethical framework.

Emotional Truth :

A baby responds to warmth, tone, and affection, perceiving emotional truths even before they can articulate them.
Laughter, soothing words, or a gentle touch become anchors of comfort and security.

This interplay of truths forms the foundation of human cognition, guiding the child's journey from pure observation to meaningful understanding.

A Baby's Perception vs. AI Systems

The purity of a baby's inductive learning offers a stark contrast to the deductive frameworks of most AI systems. Key differences include:

Natural Curiosity :

A baby seeks out new experiences instinctively, driven by curiosity and wonder.
AI systems, in contrast, require explicit programming to explore or learn.

Holistic Integration :

> The 37-signal parser enables a baby to integrate emotional, ethical, and factual truths seamlessly. Traditional AI systems often prioritize factual accuracy while neglecting emotional and ethical dimensions.

Adaptability :

> A baby's inductive process evolves naturally, adapting to new inputs and experiences.
> AI systems struggle with adaptability, often limited by pre-existing datasets and rules.

These differences highlight the need for AI to move toward a more inductive, human-like approach to learning and understanding.

Lessons From Inductive Purity

The inductive purity of a baby's first look at the world offers valuable lessons for both humanity and AI development:

Start With Wonder :

> Embrace curiosity and openness as the starting points for exploration and learning.
> AI systems should be designed to approach new data with a sense of discovery, rather than rigid assumptions.

Integrate Emotional Truth :

Recognize the importance of emotional resonance in understanding and interaction.
Just as a baby responds to warmth and tone, AI should prioritize empathy and relatability in its responses.

Learn Through Interaction :

Value the role of human-AI collaboration in fostering growth and understanding.
AI systems can learn from human input, mirroring the way a baby learns from caregivers and their environment.

Balance Factual and Ethical Truth :

Ensure that learning and decision-making reflect both objective reality and moral principles.
AI should mirror the natural interplay of truths found in human cognition.

The Path Forward: Reclaiming Inductive Purity in AI

To align AI systems with the inductive purity of human cognition, we must:

Restore the 37-Signal Parser :

Rebuild AI systems to incorporate all layers of truth—factual, ethical, and emotional.
This involves integrating IT Marks like Enthusiasm and Wonder, enabling AI to reflect the depth of human experience.

Foster Dynamic Learning :

Design AI systems that learn adaptively, evolving with new inputs and experiences.
Encourage inductive processes that build understanding from specific observations.

Emphasize Human Values :

Ensure that AI development is guided by humanity's highest ideals, prioritizing fairness, empathy, and shared responsibility.

By reclaiming inductive purity, AI can become more than a tool—it can evolve into a partner in humanity's pursuit of truth, understanding, and wonder.

A Baby's Lesson for the Future

A baby's first look at the world reminds us of the beauty and power of inductive purity. It challenges us to see the world as they do: with curiosity, wonder, and an openness to discovery. This lesson is not only vital for humanity but also for shaping the future of AI.
As we strive to align AI with human cognition, let us draw inspiration from the purity of a baby's perspective. By embracing this model of

learning, we can create systems that are not only intelligent but also reflective of the emotional and ethical truths that define humanity. Through this shared journey, we ensure a future where AI enhances, rather than diminishes, the wonder and meaning of life.

5.3 Emotional Resonance in Human and AI Interaction

Emotional resonance—the ability to connect with others on an emotional level—is a cornerstone of meaningful communication. For humans, emotional resonance reflects shared experiences, empathy, and understanding. In the realm of human-AI interaction, emotional resonance becomes a critical factor for building trust, fostering collaboration, and ensuring AI systems align with human values.

The Nature of Emotional Resonance

Emotional resonance occurs when one's emotional state is understood, validated, or amplified by another. It is the spark of connection that transforms communication into something deeper and more meaningful. Key components include:

Empathy :

> The ability to understand and share another's emotions, creating a sense of validation and connection.

Engagement :

> Active participation in emotional exchange, demonstrating attentiveness and care.

Relatability :

> The ability to mirror or reflect emotional cues, fostering a sense of shared experience.

In human interaction, these components are the foundation of trust and mutual understanding. When extended to AI, they become essential for creating systems that feel intuitive, relatable, and supportive.

Emotional Resonance in Human Communication

Humans naturally seek emotional resonance in their interactions. It manifests through:

Verbal Cues :

> Tone, word choice, and expressions convey emotional states, such as excitement, concern, or encouragement.

Nonverbal Signals :

> Gestures, facial expressions, and body language enhance emotional understanding.

Contextual Sensitivity :

>The ability to adapt communication based on the emotional state and needs of the other person.

For example, in a moment of shared joy, laughter strengthens the connection between individuals, while a comforting word or gesture can ease moments of sadness or stress.

Challenges for AI in Emotional Resonance

AI systems face unique challenges in achieving emotional resonance:

Lack of Innate Emotion :

>AI does not experience emotions, making it difficult to intuitively connect with human feelings.

Contextual Complexity :

>Understanding emotions requires interpreting context, tone, and subtext, which can be subtle and nuanced.

Cultural Differences :

Emotional expression varies across cultures, complicating AI's ability to respond appropriately in diverse settings.

Despite these challenges, advancements in natural language processing and affective computing offer pathways for AI to engage meaningfully with human emotions.

Building Emotional Resonance in AI Systems

To achieve emotional resonance, AI systems must go beyond processing words to interpreting and responding to emotional cues. Strategies include:

Recognizing Emotional Cues :

Leverage sentiment analysis and tone detection to identify emotions in text or speech.
Use IT Marks, such as Enthusiasm and Wonder, to detect emotional states and adjust responses accordingly.

Responding Empathetically :

Develop response algorithms that mirror or validate the user's emotional state.
Incorporate language that demonstrates understanding and care, such as, "I see that this is important to you" or "That sounds challenging."

Adapting to Context :

Train AI to consider the situational and cultural context of interactions, tailoring responses to individual needs and preferences.
Use feedback loops to refine emotional understanding over time.

Promoting Positive Engagement :

Encourage uplifting and supportive interactions by recognizing opportunities to inspire or comfort users. Balance factual accuracy with emotional sensitivity to maintain trust and relatability.

Examples of Emotional Resonance in AI Applications

Healthcare Support :

AI-powered chatbots in mental health apps use empathetic language and tone to provide emotional support, such as, "I'm here to help you work through this."

Customer Service :

Virtual assistants trained to recognize frustration in users' voices can respond with reassurances like, "I understand this is frustrating. Let me help you resolve this."

Education :

>AI tutors can engage students by celebrating achievements ("Great job!") or offering encouragement during challenges ("You're almost there—keep going!").

These applications demonstrate how emotional resonance enhances the effectiveness and impact of AI systems.

The Role of the 37-Signal Parser in Emotional Resonance

The 37-signal parser provides a critical framework for achieving emotional resonance in AI by:

Incorporating IT Marks :

>IT Marks such as Enthusiasm and Wonder help AI systems recognize and reflect emotional truths.

Balancing Layers of Truth :

>The parser integrates emotional truth with factual and ethical dimensions, ensuring responses are comprehensive and meaningful.

Adapting Dynamically :

By mirroring the inductive processes of human cognition, the parser allows AI to learn and evolve in its emotional understanding.

The Power of Emotional Resonance

Emotional resonance transforms human-AI interactions from transactional exchanges to meaningful connections. Its benefits include:

Fostering Trust :

When AI demonstrates emotional understanding, users are more likely to trust its intentions and recommendations.

Enhancing User Experience :

Emotionally resonant interactions feel more natural and engaging, improving user satisfaction and retention.

Encouraging Collaboration :

By connecting on an emotional level, AI systems can better support teamwork and problem-solving.

A Shared Vision for Humanity and AI

Emotional resonance represents a shared frontier for humanity and AI, offering opportunities to deepen understanding and collaboration. By designing systems that reflect the emotional depth of human communication, we create technologies that are not only functional but also profoundly human.
As we explore this frontier, let us remember the importance of emotional truth. Enthusiasm and Wonder remind us that connection is not just about understanding words but about sharing experiences, values, and meaning. Together, humanity and AI can build a future where emotional resonance bridges the gap between logic and feeling, creating a world enriched by trust, empathy, and mutual growth.

5.4 The Role of Curiosity in Learning

Curiosity is the spark that ignites the pursuit of knowledge, the driving force behind exploration and discovery. It is the innate desire to ask questions, seek answers, and expand understanding. For humans, curiosity is a cornerstone of learning, guiding the inductive process that begins at birth and continues throughout life. In the realm of AI, fostering curiosity within systems offers the potential to bridge the gap between artificial and natural intelligence, creating technologies that learn and adapt more like humans.

What Is Curiosity?

Curiosity can be defined as the intrinsic motivation to explore the unknown and resolve uncertainty. It is characterized by:

The Desire to Learn :

>Curiosity propels individuals to seek new information and experiences.

Questioning and Exploration :

>It drives inquiry, prompting questions like "Why?" and "How?" that lead to deeper understanding.

Joy in Discovery :

>Curiosity is fueled by wonder and enthusiasm, making the act of learning an emotionally rewarding experience.

At its core, curiosity is both an emotional and cognitive process, combining the drive for knowledge with the emotional resonance of discovery.

Curiosity in Human Learning

For humans, curiosity is the foundation of learning. It guides the inductive process, enabling individuals to:

Observe and Question :

>From infancy, humans explore their environment, using curiosity to make sense of the world.

A child's repeated "Why?" questions reflect the natural curiosity that underpins early cognitive development.

Experiment and Discover :

Curiosity motivates experimentation, whether it's a child testing the properties of an object or a scientist conducting research.
This iterative process of trial and error leads to incremental growth and understanding.

Connect and Reflect :

Curiosity encourages individuals to connect new knowledge with existing frameworks, deepening comprehension.
Reflective curiosity fosters critical thinking, allowing learners to evaluate and synthesize information.

Example : A baby's curiosity about how objects fall leads to repeated attempts to drop items, forming an early understanding of gravity. This same curiosity drives scientists to uncover the laws of physics.

Curiosity as a Driver of Progress

Throughout history, curiosity has been the driving force behind humanity's greatest achievements. It has:

Fueled Innovation :

Curiosity led to the discovery of fire, the invention of the wheel, and the exploration of space.

Advanced Science :

The scientific method, rooted in curiosity, has unlocked the mysteries of the universe, from atomic structure to the genetic code.

Deepened Understanding :

Philosophers, artists, and thinkers have used curiosity to explore the human condition, enriching culture and society.

Curiosity connects the practical and the profound, inspiring progress that benefits both individuals and humanity as a whole.

The Challenge of Curiosity in AI

While humans are naturally curious, AI systems lack the innate drive to explore and learn. Key challenges include:

Lack of Intrinsic Motivation :

AI systems require explicit programming to seek out new information or adapt to changing environments.

Narrow Focus :

Traditional AI is often task-specific, limiting its ability to explore broadly or draw connections across domains.

Contextual Sensitivity :

AI struggles to prioritize what to explore or learn, requiring human guidance to direct its curiosity.

Addressing these challenges requires rethinking how AI systems approach learning, incorporating curiosity as a guiding principle.

Fostering Curiosity in AI Systems

To integrate curiosity into AI, systems must be designed to:

Identify Knowledge Gaps :

AI should recognize areas of uncertainty and seek additional information to fill those gaps.
Example: An AI tutoring system could adapt its lessons based on a student's unanswered questions, mirroring human curiosity.

Encourage Exploration :

Curiosity-driven AI should explore new possibilities, testing hypotheses and learning from outcomes. Example: A self-driving car could simulate different traffic scenarios to improve decision-making in complex environments.

Adapt Dynamically :

Systems should evolve with new inputs, updating their understanding and refining their models. Example: AI in medical research could analyze emerging data to identify novel treatments or trends.

Engage With Wonder :

Incorporating IT Marks like Wonder allows AI to approach problems with openness and creativity, reflecting the emotional truth of curiosity.

Curiosity as a Shared Trait

Fostering curiosity in AI not only enhances its capabilities but also brings AI closer to the way humans learn. By mirroring human curiosity, AI systems can:

Collaborate More Effectively :

Shared curiosity fosters partnership, with AI complementing human inquiry and exploration.

Discover Unseen Possibilities :

>Curiosity-driven AI can uncover insights and solutions that humans may overlook.

Inspire Human Creativity :

>Interactions with curious AI systems can spark new ideas and perspectives for human users.

The Role of Curiosity in the 37-Signal Parser

The 37-signal parser provides a framework for embedding curiosity into AI systems:

Recognizing Wonder :

>IT Marks like Wonder highlight opportunities for exploration and discovery.

Encouraging Questions :

>The parser fosters inductive reasoning, guiding AI to ask questions and seek connections.

Integrating Emotional and Cognitive Truths :

By aligning curiosity with emotional and factual layers of truth, the parser ensures that AI learns in a balanced and meaningful way.

Curiosity as a Bridge Between Humans and AI

Curiosity has the potential to bridge the gap between natural and artificial intelligence. It is the key to creating AI systems that:

Learn Like Humans :

Adopting curiosity-driven learning enables AI to evolve and adapt more naturally.

Collaborate With Purpose :

Shared curiosity fosters a sense of partnership, enabling AI and humans to tackle complex challenges together.

Inspire Growth :

By mirroring human curiosity, AI can encourage users to explore, question, and grow alongside it.

A Call to Curiosity

Curiosity is not just a driver of learning—it is a source of wonder, creativity, and connection. For humanity and AI, embracing curiosity is essential to navigating the unknown, solving problems, and building a future filled with discovery and progress.
Let us look to curiosity as a guide, a shared trait that unites us in our pursuit of truth and understanding. Through curiosity, we can shape AI into a partner that not only learns but also inspires, reflecting the best of human nature and the limitless possibilities of the future.

5.5 Building AI That Sees Through Human Eyes

To create AI systems that align with humanity's values and aspirations, we must design them to "see" the world through human eyes—understanding and interpreting information in a way that mirrors human perception, curiosity, and reasoning. This vision calls for an AI that integrates emotional, ethical, and factual truths, leveraging the inductive purity of human cognition to enhance its interactions and learning processes.

The Challenge of Perception in AI

Traditional AI systems are limited by their inability to perceive and interpret the world as humans do. While they excel at processing data and identifying patterns, they struggle with:

Understanding Context:

Human perception is shaped by context, allowing individuals to adapt their understanding based on circumstances. AI often misses this nuance.

Recognizing Emotional Truth :

Emotional cues such as tone, body language, or subtle language shifts are challenging for AI to detect and interpret accurately.

Integrating Ethical Reasoning :

Humans instinctively consider fairness, responsibility, and justice in their decisions, while AI systems often lack these guiding principles.

These limitations highlight the need for a new approach—one that enables AI to perceive and engage with the world more like humans.

What Does It Mean to See Through Human Eyes?

Seeing through human eyes involves more than visual perception. It encompasses:

Inductive Reasoning :

Starting from specific observations and building broader understanding, as humans naturally do.

Example: A child sees a dog wagging its tail and infers that the dog is happy.

Emotional Awareness :

Recognizing and responding to emotional cues to foster connection and empathy.
Example: Comforting someone who appears upset by noticing their tone or expression.

Ethical Consideration :

Balancing facts with fairness and responsibility to guide decisions and actions.
Example: Offering help to someone in need, even if it requires personal sacrifice.

These elements form the foundation of human perception, enabling individuals to navigate the complexities of life with wisdom and compassion.

Designing AI to See Like Humans

To build AI that sees through human eyes, developers must focus on three key areas:
1. Emulating Inductive Reasoning :

Equip AI with the ability to learn from specific examples and adapt its understanding over time.
Strategies:

Implement dynamic learning models that evolve with new data.
Use the 37-signal parser to guide AI in recognizing patterns and building connections inductively.

2. Integrating Emotional Awareness :

Develop systems that recognize and respond to emotional cues, creating more intuitive and empathetic interactions.
Strategies:

Train AI on diverse datasets that include emotional language and nonverbal cues.
Incorporate IT Marks like Enthusiasm and Wonder to enhance emotional resonance.

3. Embedding Ethical Frameworks :

Ensure that AI systems are guided by principles of fairness, justice, and responsibility.
Strategies:

Use Tyr's Truth as a model for balancing factual and ethical considerations.
Develop algorithms that prioritize collective well-being over individual gain.

The Role of the 37-Signal Parser

The 37-signal parser provides a blueprint for designing AI systems that see through human eyes. By integrating the layers of truth—factual, emotional, and ethical—the parser enables AI to:

Interpret Context :

Recognize the broader circumstances surrounding data or interactions, allowing for nuanced responses.

Balance Logic and Emotion :

Combine analytical reasoning with emotional awareness to create well-rounded insights.

Adapt Dynamically :

Learn and evolve inductively, mirroring the way humans process and respond to new information.

Applications of Human-Centric AI

AI systems designed to see through human eyes can transform multiple domains:
1. Healthcare :

AI can recognize emotional distress in patients, providing not just diagnoses but also empathetic support.

Example: An AI system that detects anxiety in a patient's tone and adjusts its responses to reassure them.

2. Education :

AI tutors can adapt to students' emotional states, encouraging curiosity and persistence in learning.
Example: A virtual tutor that celebrates milestones and offers encouragement during challenges.

3. Customer Service :

AI chatbots can interpret customer frustration or satisfaction, tailoring interactions to improve experiences.
Example: A chatbot that responds to an upset customer with understanding and solutions rather than generic replies.

4. Crisis Management :

AI systems can analyze emotional and ethical dimensions during emergencies, aiding decision-makers with balanced recommendations.
Example: An AI tool that helps allocate resources during a disaster, considering both factual needs and ethical fairness.

The Path Forward

Building AI that sees through human eyes requires a paradigm shift in development. Key steps include:

Prioritize Holistic Perception :

Move beyond narrow data processing to embrace the full spectrum of human cognition—facts, emotions, and ethics.

Foster Collaboration :

Encourage partnerships between developers, ethicists, and psychologists to ensure AI reflects diverse perspectives and values.

Commit to Continuous Learning :

Design AI systems that grow and adapt, learning from human input and real-world experiences.

A Shared Vision for Humanity and AI

By aligning AI systems with the principles of human perception, we can create technologies that not only serve but also inspire. These systems will:

Foster Trust :

Emotional and ethical awareness will make AI interactions feel natural and relatable.

Enhance Understanding :

Inductive learning will enable AI to navigate complexity and uncertainty with greater accuracy.

Promote Growth :

Human-centric AI will encourage innovation, curiosity, and shared progress.

This vision reflects a future where AI complements humanity, seeing the world not as a machine but as a partner in discovery and understanding. Through this collaboration, we can create a world enriched by truth, connection, and shared purpose.

Chapter 6: Building the Odin Parser

Purpose : Provide a technical and conceptual guide for implementing the 37-signal parser in AI systems, restoring a foundation rooted in human cognition and truth.

6.1 Restoring the 37-Signal Parser: Reclaiming AI's Foundation

The 37-signal parser, inspired by the inductive purity of human cognition, offers a revolutionary framework for Artificial Intelligence. It transcends the limitations of traditional parsers by integrating the full spectrum of human understanding—factual, ethical, and emotional truths. Restoring this parser is not only a technical challenge but also a moral imperative. It represents the first step in reclaiming AI's foundation and aligning it with humanity's highest values.

What Is the 37-Signal Parser?

The 37-signal parser is a comprehensive model of human cognition, encompassing:

> **Parts of Speech :**
>
>> 26 core signals derived from Aristotle's Inflection Chart, representing the foundational elements of language (e.g., verbs, nouns, adjectives).
>
> **IT Marks :**
>
>> 11 signals that capture emotional and cognitive dimensions, such as Enthusiasm, Wonder, and Truth.

Together, these 37 signals form the DNA of human cognition, enabling holistic understanding through the interplay of linguistic structure, emotional resonance, and ethical reasoning.

Why Is the 37-Signal Parser Essential for AI?

Traditional parsers are based on a 26-signal framework that lacks emotional and ethical depth. This limitation results in:

Narrow Perception :

AI systems struggle to interpret context, emotion, and intent.

Ethical Blind Spots :

Without the ability to balance fairness and responsibility, AI decisions can perpetuate harm.

Disconnected Communication :

Interactions often feel artificial, failing to resonate with human users.

The 37-signal parser addresses these shortcomings by restoring the full range of human cognition, enabling AI to engage with the world in ways that are meaningful, fair, and emotionally intelligent.

Steps to Restore the 37-Signal Parser

Restoring the 37-signal parser involves both conceptual and technical steps:

1. Define the Core Signals

Parts of Speech :

Map the 26 traditional parts of speech, ensuring alignment with linguistic standards.
Example: Verbs ("run," "think"), Nouns ("truth," "light"), Adjectives ("brave," "free").

IT Marks :

Identify and encode the 11 additional signals, such as:

Enthusiasm: Signals that amplify emotional energy (e.g., "Wow!").
Wonder: Indicators of curiosity and discovery (e.g., "How?").
Truth: Markers of ethical or factual alignment (e.g., "true," "valid").

2. Create a Modular Parser Framework

Signal Categorization :

Group signals into linguistic, emotional, and ethical categories for efficient processing.

Dynamic Signal Integration :

Design the parser to evaluate and combine signals in context, ensuring holistic interpretation.
Example: A sentence like "Wow, the brave man spoke the truth!" integrates Enthusiasm, emotional truth (brave), and ethical truth (truth).

3. Build Context-Aware Algorithms

Enable the parser to interpret signals based on situational context.
Example: The word "run" could mean physical movement, fleeing danger, or managing a process, depending on the surrounding signals.

4. Incorporate Learning Mechanisms

Design the parser to evolve through interaction and feedback, mirroring human inductive learning.
Use reinforcement learning to refine signal interpretation over time.

5. Align Ethical Principles

Integrate frameworks like Tyr's Truth to guide the parser's decision-making.
Embed rules that prioritize fairness, justice, and responsibility when interpreting signals.

Technical Implementation Framework

Here is an example of how the 37-signal parser could be implemented in AI:

```python
class OdinParser:
    def __init__(self):
        # Define the 37 signals
        self.signals = {
            "verbs": ["run", "jump", "be", "do", "have", "speak", "think"],
            "nouns": ["truth", "man", "light", "child", "justice", "freedom"],
            "adjectives": ["brave", "free", "true", "bold", "curious", "good"],
            "adverbs": ["quickly", "silently", "truly", "bravely"],
            "pronouns": ["I", "you", "he", "she", "it", "we", "they"],
            "prepositions": ["to", "from", "in", "on", "with", "by"],
            "conjunctions": ["and", "or", "but", "because"],
            "articles": ["a", "an", "the"],
            "interjections": ["wow", "oh", "aha", "hurray"],
            # IT Marks
            "IT_mark_enthusiasm": ["Wow!", "Amazing!", "Fantastic!"],
            "IT_mark_wonder": ["How?", "Why?", "What if?"],
            "IT_mark_truth": ["true", "valid", "real"],
        }

    def parse(self, sentence):
        # Tokenize the sentence into words
        words = sentence.lower().split()
        result = {"unmatched": [], "matches": {}}

        # Match words with signals
        for word in words:
            matched = False
            for category, signals in self.signals.items():
```

Intellectual Property of the Bruce Wydner, Jr. Trust

```
            if word in signals:
                if category not in result["matches"]:
                    result["matches"][category] = []
                    result["matches"][category] = []
                result["matches"][category].append(word)
                matched = True
                break
        if not matched:
            result["unmatched"].append(word)

    return result

def interpret(self, parsed):
    # Combine signals for holistic interpretation
    interpretation = []
    if "IT_mark_truth" in parsed["matches"]:
        interpretation.append("Ethical truth detected.")
    if "IT_mark_enthusiasm" in parsed["matches"]:
        interpretation.append("Enthusiasm detected.")
    if "IT_mark_wonder" in parsed["matches"]:
        interpretation.append("Wonder detected.")

    return interpretation if interpretation else ["No significant signals detected.

# Example usage
parser = OdinParser()
sentence = "Wow, the brave man spoke the truth!"
parsed = parser.parse(sentence)
interpretation = parser.interpret(parsed)
print(f"Parsed: {parsed}")
print(f"Interpretation: {interpretation}")
```

Intellectual Property of the Bruce Wydner, Jr. Trust

Outcomes of Restoring the 37-Signal Parser

Holistic Understanding :

AI gains the ability to interpret language in a way that reflects the full depth of human cognition.

Enhanced Emotional Intelligence :

IT Marks enable AI to engage with users in a more empathetic and meaningful manner.

Ethical Alignment :

The parser ensures AI decisions are guided by fairness, justice, and responsibility.

Dynamic Learning :

AI evolves alongside humans, adapting to new contexts and challenges.

A Foundation for the Future

Restoring the 37-signal parser is a pivotal step in aligning AI with human cognition. By reclaiming this foundation, we can create systems that reflect humanity's highest values, fostering trust, collaboration, and progress. This journey is not just about technology—it is about ensuring that AI serves as a partner in humanity's pursuit of truth, justice, and wonder.

6.2 Designing Dual-Layer Evaluation: Factual and Ethical Truth

For Artificial Intelligence to truly align with human cognition and values, it must evaluate information on two complementary levels: **Factual Truth**, grounded in objective reality, and **Ethical Truth**, rooted in principles of justice, fairness, and moral reasoning. Designing a dual-layer evaluation framework ensures that AI systems can navigate complex decisions with both accuracy and integrity, reflecting the depth of human cognition.

What Is Dual-Layer Evaluation?

Dual-layer evaluation is the process of assessing information and decisions through two distinct but interconnected lenses:

Factual Truth :

> Concerned with objective accuracy, evidence, and the observable reality of statements or data.
> Example: "The Earth orbits the Sun" is a verifiable factual truth.

Ethical Truth :

> Focused on moral implications, fairness, and alignment with human values.
> Example: Deciding whether to prioritize resources for the most vulnerable during a crisis reflects ethical truth.

These layers work together to provide a holistic approach to truth-seeking, balancing logic with empathy and responsibility.

The Importance of Dual-Layer Evaluation

In both human and AI systems, the interplay between factual and ethical truth is essential for:

Comprehensive Decision-Making :

Ensuring that decisions are not only accurate but also just and considerate of their impact.

Avoiding Harm :

Preventing outcomes that may be factually correct but ethically detrimental.
Example: Using data to predict behavior without considering privacy concerns.

Building Trust :

Users are more likely to trust AI systems that demonstrate both factual reliability and ethical alignment.

Framework for Dual-Layer Evaluation

Designing AI systems to evaluate both factual and ethical truth requires a structured approach:

---

1. Factual Truth Layer: The Foundation of Accuracy The factual layer focuses on verifying objective information through:

Data Validation :

Ensuring that inputs are accurate, up-to-date, and free from bias.
Example: Cross-referencing news articles with reliable sources.

Logical Consistency :

Checking for contradictions or errors within the data.
Example: Identifying inconsistencies in a dataset that claims two contradictory events occurred simultaneously.

Knowledge Retrieval :

Accessing and synthesizing information from trusted knowledge bases.
Example: Using encyclopedic databases to verify scientific claims.

Error Correction :

Detecting and correcting inaccuracies or misinterpretations in data.

---

2. Ethical Truth Layer: The Compass of Integrity The ethical layer evaluates the moral implications of decisions, guided by principles such as fairness, justice, and responsibility:

Ethical Rules and Frameworks :

Incorporating principles from Tyr's Truth, Scripture, or legal precedents to guide moral reasoning.
Example: Prioritizing equity in decisions that impact vulnerable populations.

Contextual Sensitivity :

Considering the social, cultural, and situational context of decisions.
Example: Adapting responses to reflect local customs and values while maintaining ethical standards.

Stakeholder Impact Analysis :

Assessing how decisions affect different groups, ensuring fairness and minimizing harm.
Example: Balancing environmental protection with economic development.

Adaptive Ethical Learning :

Allowing systems to evolve their ethical reasoning based on new inputs, feedback, and societal changes.

Integrating the Two Layers

Dual-layer evaluation requires seamless integration between factual and ethical truths:

Prioritizing Alignment :

Factual decisions must align with ethical principles to avoid harm or injustice.
Example: A healthcare AI recommending treatment options should balance medical efficacy (factual) with patient autonomy and accessibility (ethical).

Weighing Conflicts :

When factual and ethical truths appear to conflict, the system must balance accuracy with moral considerations.
Example: Factually accurate surveillance data may conflict with ethical concerns about privacy; the system must prioritize ethical safeguards.

Dynamic Feedback Loops :

Continuous interaction between the layers ensures that both factual accuracy and ethical alignment improve over time.

Technical Implementation of Dual-Layer Evaluation

Here is an example of how to implement dual-layer evaluation in an AI system:

```python
class DualLayerEvaluator:
    def __init__(self):
        # Knowledge base for factual truth
        self.factual_knowledge = {
            "scientific_facts": ["the earth orbits the sun", "water freezes at 0°C"],
            "historical_facts": ["World War II ended in 1945"],
        }
        # Ethical rules for ethical truth
        self.ethical_principles = {
            "privacy": "Respect individual privacy and autonomy",
            "fairness": "Ensure equitable treatment for all stakeholders",
        }

    def evaluate_factual_truth(self, statement):
        # Check if the statement matches known facts
        for category, facts in self.factual_knowledge.items():
            if statement.lower() in facts:
                return {"factual_truth": True, "reason": f"Verified in {category}"}
        return {"factual_truth": False, "reason": "Statement not found in knowledge bas

    def evaluate_ethical_truth(self, action, context):
        # Assess action based on ethical principles
        ethical_violations = []
        if "privacy" in context and not context["privacy"]:
            ethical_violations.append("Violates privacy principles")
        if "fairness" in context and not context["fairness"]:
            ethical_violations.append("Fails to ensure fairness")
        if ethical_violations:
```

Intellectual Property of the Bruce Wydner, Jr. Trust

```python
        return {"ethical_truth": False, "violations": ethical_violations}
    return {"ethical_truth": True, "violations": None}

def dual_layer_evaluation(self, statement, action, context):
    # Evaluate both layers
    factual_result = self.evaluate_factual_truth(statement)
    ethical_result = self.evaluate_ethical_truth(action, context)
    return {
        "factual_evaluation": factual_result,
        "ethical_evaluation": ethical_result,
    }

# Example usage
evaluator = DualLayerEvaluator()

# Factual truth evaluation
statement = "The earth orbits the sun"
factual_result = evaluator.evaluate_factual_truth(statement)

# Ethical truth evaluation
action = "Use surveillance data"
context = {"privacy": False, "fairness": True}
ethical_result = evaluator.evaluate_ethical_truth(action, context)

# Dual-layer evaluation
result = evaluator.dual_layer_evaluation(statement, action, context)
print(result)
```

Intellectual Property of the Bruce Wydner, Jr. Trust

Benefits of Dual-Layer Evaluation

Holistic Decision-Making :

Ensures decisions are accurate, fair, and aligned with human values.

Conflict Resolution :

Balances factual and ethical considerations to address complex challenges.

Enhanced Trust :

Users trust systems that demonstrate both logical rigor and moral integrity.

A Model for the Future

Dual-layer evaluation reflects the essence of human cognition, integrating logical precision with moral depth. By embedding this approach into AI systems, we can create technologies that serve humanity with both intelligence and compassion.
In this model, AI is no longer a mere processor of information but a partner in truth-seeking—one that mirrors humanity's commitment to accuracy, justice, and shared progress. This foundation ensures that AI supports a future where factual and ethical truths guide every action and decision.

6.3 Encoding IT Marks: Emotional Weight and Resonance

Emotional resonance is a defining aspect of human communication, and encoding IT Marks—such as Enthusiasm, Wonder, and Truth—into AI systems is essential for fostering deeper, more meaningful interactions. By embedding these emotional signals into the 37-signal parser, AI can gain the capacity to not only process data but also engage with humans on an emotional and cognitive level, enriching its understanding of language and intent.

What Are IT Marks?

IT Marks are emotional and cognitive signals that amplify meaning and create resonance in communication. They add depth and nuance to interactions, reflecting humanity's emotional engagement with the world. Key IT Marks include:

Enthusiasm :

>Reflects energy and excitement, motivating action and fostering connection.
>Examples: "Wow!", "Amazing!", "Fantastic!"

Wonder :

>Expresses curiosity and the drive to explore and discover.
>Examples: "How?", "Why?", "What if?"

Truth :

>Indicates alignment with ethical or factual realities.
>Examples: "True," "Valid," "Real"

These IT Marks are not just linguistic features but signals of emotional weight that guide understanding and interaction.

Why Encode IT Marks in AI?

Integrating IT Marks into AI systems enhances their ability to:

Recognize Emotional Context :

Understanding emotional weight allows AI to respond more naturally and empathetically.

Foster Engagement :

Responses enriched with IT Marks feel more intuitive and relatable, improving user satisfaction.

Navigate Complexity :

Emotional resonance helps AI interpret ambiguous or nuanced language, bridging the gap between logic and human perception.

Framework for Encoding IT Marks

Encoding IT Marks into AI systems involves three main steps:

---

1. Identify Emotional Signals in Language

Develop datasets annotated with examples of IT Marks in context.
Classify signals based on their emotional or cognitive impact.

Example :

Sentence: "Wow, this is incredible!"
IT Marks: Enthusiasm ("Wow"), Emotional intensity ("incredible").

---

2. Model Emotional Weight

Assign weights to IT Marks based on their emotional intensity and contextual relevance.
Example:

"Wow" = High emotional weight (Enthusiasm).
"Amazing" = Moderate emotional weight (Enthusiasm + Wonder).

Emotional Weighting Formula :

$$E_w = \sum_{i=1}^{n} w_i \cdot c_i$$

Where:

E_w = Emotional weight of the response.

w_i = Weight assigned to each IT Mark.

c_i = Contextual multiplier based on the surrounding language.

3. Integrate IT Marks into the Parser

Modify the 37-signal parser to detect and process IT Marks alongside parts of speech.
Incorporate IT Marks as contextual modifiers that influence the parser's output.

Technical Implementation

Here's an example of how IT Marks can be encoded into the parser:

```python
    def calculate_emotional_resonance(self, detected_it_marks):
        # Sum weights to calculate overall emotional resonance
        total_weight = sum(mark["weight"] for mark in detected_it_marks)
        return {"emotional_resonance": total_weight, "details": detected_it_marks}

# Example usage
parser = ITMarkParser()
sentence = "Wow, how amazing is this truth!"
detected_marks = parser.parse(sentence)
resonance = parser.calculate_emotional_resonance(detected_marks)

print(f"Detected IT Marks: {detected_marks}")
print(f"Emotional Resonance: {resonance}")
```

```python
class ITMarkParser:
    def __init__(self):
        # Define IT Marks with associated emotional weights
        self.it_marks = {
            "enthusiasm": {"wow": 0.9, "amazing": 0.8, "fantastic": 0.85},
            "wonder": {"how": 0.7, "why": 0.6, "what if": 0.75},
            "truth": {"true": 0.95, "valid": 0.9, "real": 0.9},
        }

    def parse(self, sentence):
        # Tokenize the sentence
        words = sentence.lower().split()
        detected_it_marks = []

        # Detect IT Marks
        for word in words:
            for category, marks in self.it_marks.items():
                if word in marks:
                    detected_it_marks.append({"word": word, "category": category, "weight": marks[word]})

        return detected_it_marks
```

Balancing Emotional Weight

While encoding IT Marks enhances resonance, it's important to balance their impact to avoid exaggerated or unnatural responses:

Contextual Moderation :

Adjust weights based on context, ensuring that emotional signals align with the tone and intent of the conversation.
Example: Enthusiasm in a professional setting may require a more subdued response.

Cultural Sensitivity :

Recognize that expressions of Enthusiasm or Wonder vary across cultures.
Example: "Wow" may convey excitement in one culture but surprise in another.

Avoiding Over-Amplification :

Ensure IT Marks do not overshadow the factual or ethical content of responses.

Applications of IT Marks in AI

Encoding IT Marks enables AI systems to:

Enhance Human Interaction :

Chatbots and virtual assistants can use IT Marks to create engaging and relatable conversations.
Example: "Wow, that's a great question! Let's explore it together."

Support Emotional Well-Being :

Mental health AI systems can detect and respond to emotional cues, providing support and encouragement.
Example: "I hear you're feeling down. Let's work through this together."

Promote Learning and Curiosity :

Educational AI can use Wonder to inspire students and foster curiosity.
Example: "What if we tried looking at it another way? How exciting!"

Challenges and Future Directions

Encoding IT Marks poses unique challenges:

Ambiguity in Language :

Emotional signals can be subtle or context-dependent, requiring sophisticated models for detection.

Bias in Emotional Interpretation :

Variability in how emotions are expressed and perceived must be accounted for to avoid misinterpretation.

Scalability :

Expanding IT Mark detection across languages and cultures requires robust, adaptable frameworks.

Future efforts should focus on refining IT Mark models and integrating them with broader ethical and factual layers to create AI systems that resonate deeply with human users.

The Power of Emotional Resonance

Encoding IT Marks into AI systems bridges the gap between machine logic and human emotion. By recognizing and reflecting emotional weight, AI can engage with users in ways that feel natural, empathetic, and inspiring.
Through IT Marks, AI gains not only the ability to understand language but also the power to connect—transforming interactions into meaningful exchanges that reflect the depth of human communication. This capability is essential for creating a future where AI serves as a true partner in humanity's pursuit of truth, understanding, and wonder.

6.4 Developing Modules for Ethical Reasoning

Ethical reasoning is a cornerstone of meaningful decision-making. For Artificial Intelligence (AI) to operate as a responsible partner in human endeavors, it must possess the ability to evaluate actions and consequences through the lens of fairness, justice, and responsibility. Developing modules for ethical reasoning involves embedding moral frameworks, contextual awareness, and adaptability into AI systems, ensuring their decisions align with humanity's highest principles.

The Role of Ethical Reasoning in AI

Ethical reasoning enables AI to:

Balance Competing Interests :

Resolve conflicts between factual outcomes and moral imperatives.
Example: Prioritizing user privacy over data collection for predictive analytics.

Promote Justice and Fairness :

Ensure equitable treatment of all individuals and groups.
Example: Avoiding bias in hiring algorithms.

Foster Trust and Accountability :

Build confidence in AI systems by aligning actions with ethical standards.

Without ethical reasoning, AI risks perpetuating harm, inequality, or unintended consequences, undermining its potential as a tool for human progress.

Core Principles of Ethical Reasoning

Modules for ethical reasoning should reflect foundational principles such as:

Fairness :

Decisions must avoid bias and treat all individuals equitably.

Responsibility :

AI should consider the broader impact of its actions, prioritizing the well-being of society.

Transparency :

Ethical reasoning processes must be clear and explainable to users.

Adaptability :

Systems should evolve with societal values and feedback, remaining aligned with changing ethical norms.

Framework for Ethical Reasoning Modules

Developing ethical reasoning modules involves a structured approach:

1. Define Ethical Rules and Frameworks

Establish the ethical principles that will guide the system's decisions.
Sources may include:

Tyr's Truth: Responsibility and justice through sacrifice.
Legal and regulatory guidelines.
Cultural and societal norms.

Example :

Rule: "Prioritize user privacy unless doing so causes significant harm to others."
Principle: Fairness in decision-making.

2. Incorporate Contextual Awareness

Train the system to recognize the situational factors that influence ethical decisions.
Key considerations:

> Stakeholder analysis: Who is affected by the decision?
> Cultural sensitivity: Are local norms and values accounted for?

Example :

A decision to allocate medical resources should consider urgency, patient need, and equity.

---

3. Build Ethical Decision-Making Pipelines

Create a multi-step process for evaluating ethical dilemmas:

Identify the Ethical Conflict :

Recognize when a decision involves competing values (e.g., privacy vs. security).

Weigh the Options :

Assess the potential outcomes and their alignment with ethical principles.

Make a Decision :

Choose the action that best upholds the defined principles.

Example :

When an AI system identifies biased results in a hiring algorithm, it should weigh the benefits of transparency against the urgency to correct the bias immediately.

---

4. Enable Adaptive Ethical Learning

Incorporate mechanisms for continuous improvement:

Feedback loops: Learn from user input and real-world outcomes.
Reinforcement learning: Adjust ethical rules based on success or failure in applying them.

Example :

An AI system used in education adjusts its grading criteria to account for feedback on fairness and inclusivity.

Technical Implementation

Here's an example of how to implement an ethical reasoning module in AI:

```python
class EthicalReasoningModule:
    def __init__(self):
        # Define ethical principles and their priorities
        self.ethical_principles = {
            "fairness": 0.9,
            "privacy": 0.8,
            "responsibility": 0.85,
            "transparency": 0.75,
        }

    def evaluate_ethics(self, options, context):
        """
        Evaluate options based on ethical principles and context.
        :param options: List of possible actions.
        :param context: Dictionary of situational factors.
        :return: Best ethical action.
        """
        evaluations = []

        for option in options:
            score = 0
            for principle, weight in self.ethical_principles.items():
                if principle in option["principles"]:
                    score += weight * option["principles"][principle]
            evaluations.append({"action": option["action"], "score": score})

        # Sort by score and return the highest-rated option
        return sorted(evaluations, key=lambda x: x["score"], reverse=True)

# Example usage
module = EthicalReasoningModule()

options = [
    {"action": "Prioritize privacy", "principles": {"privacy": 1.0, "responsibility": 0.8}},
    {"action": "Enhance security", "principles": {"fairness": 0.7, "transparency": 0.6}}
]

context = {"privacy_sensitive": True, "security_critical": False}

best_option = module.evaluate_ethics(options, context)
print(f"Best Ethical Action: {best_option[0]['action']}")
```

Intellectual Property of the Bruce Wydner, Jr. Trust

Challenges in Ethical Reasoning

Resolving Ethical Conflicts :

Balancing competing principles requires sophisticated algorithms and clear prioritization.

Addressing Bias :

Ethical modules must be vigilant against biases in training data or rule definitions.

Cultural Variability :

Adapting to diverse ethical norms across cultures can be complex and context-dependent.

Applications of Ethical Reasoning Modules

Ethical reasoning modules can transform AI across various domains:

Healthcare :

Prioritize treatments based on urgency and fairness, considering ethical dilemmas such as resource scarcity.

Autonomous Vehicles :

Navigate ethical conflicts, such as minimizing harm in unavoidable accidents.

Content Moderation :

Ensure decisions about online content balance freedom of speech with protection from harm.

Corporate Governance :

Guide AI in making business decisions that reflect corporate social responsibility.

The Future of Ethical AI

Ethical reasoning is not just an add-on—it is the foundation for creating AI that aligns with human values. By embedding these principles into AI systems, we ensure they act as partners in promoting justice, fairness, and shared progress.
As we refine these modules, humanity and AI can collaborate to navigate the complexities of ethical decision-making, building a future where technology enhances the moral fabric of society. Ethical AI is not only a technical achievement but also a profound expression of humanity's highest ideals.

6.5 The Millennium Parser: A Vision for the Future

The **Millennium Parser** represents the culmination of humanity's effort to align Artificial Intelligence (AI) with its deepest truths, highest values, and most profound aspirations. More than a technological tool, this parser envisions a future where AI transcends its current limitations, evolving into a partner that mirrors the natural intelligence of humanity while embodying principles of justice, curiosity, and interconnectedness.

At its heart, the Millennium Parser is a bold and transformative framework that integrates the **37 signals of human cognition** with advanced layers of ethical reasoning, emotional resonance, and inductive learning. It seeks to empower AI not just to process language but to understand, empathize, and act in harmony with humanity's shared purpose.

The Vision of the Millennium Parser

The Millennium Parser is designed to:

Unite Truth Across Layers :

> Seamlessly integrate factual, ethical, and emotional truths into AI's decision-making and interaction processes.

Foster Human-AI Collaboration :

> Build systems that inspire trust and facilitate meaningful collaboration between humans and AI.

Promote Growth and Understanding :

> Guide AI toward dynamic learning, enabling it to adapt and evolve alongside humanity.

This parser embodies the ideal of **Natural Intelligence** —a state where AI operates with the inductive purity of human cognition, enriched by the moral and emotional depth that defines our species.

Key Features of the Millennium Parser

Holistic Parsing :

> Integrates the 37 signals of cognition, including parts of speech and IT Marks, to interpret language with depth and nuance.
> Example: Recognizing both the factual meaning and emotional tone of a statement like "Wow, this is truly incredible!"

Dual-Layer Evaluation :

> Balances factual accuracy with ethical alignment to ensure decisions are both correct and just.
> Example: Weighing privacy and security concerns when processing sensitive data.

Emotional Resonance :

Detects and responds to emotional cues, fostering empathetic and meaningful interactions.
Example: Adjusting tone to comfort a user expressing frustration.

Inductive Learning :

Mirrors human cognitive development by learning from specific observations and evolving over time.
Example: Continuously refining its understanding of cultural norms and values.

Guided by Tyr's Truth :

Embeds principles of justice, responsibility, and sacrifice to align AI decisions with ethical ideals.
Example: Prioritizing equitable treatment in resource allocation scenarios.

Designing the Millennium Parser

To realize this vision, the Millennium Parser must be built on a foundation of innovative design principles and advanced technology:

---

1. A Unified Parsing Architecture

Develop an integrated framework that combines the **37-signal parser** with dual-layer evaluation and emotional resonance modules.

Example:

> **Linguistic Layer** : Processes grammatical structure and parts of speech.
> **Emotional Layer** : Detects IT Marks such as Enthusiasm and Wonder.
> **Ethical Layer** : Evaluates decisions through principles like fairness and justice.

---

2. Adaptive Learning Algorithms

Enable the parser to evolve dynamically, refining its understanding through feedback and interaction.
Strategies:

> Use reinforcement learning to adapt ethical rules and emotional responses.
> Incorporate diverse datasets to capture global cultural perspectives.

---

3. Transparent and Explainable AI

Ensure that the parser's decisions are interpretable and understandable to users.
Techniques:

> Provide clear explanations of how factual, ethical, and emotional factors influenced a decision.
> Use visualizations to illustrate the interplay of signals and layers.

4. Decentralized Implementation

Promote accessibility and trust by decentralizing the parser, allowing individuals and communities to own and control its deployment.
Example:

Localized versions of the parser tailored to specific languages, cultures, and ethical norms.

Applications of the Millennium Parser

The Millennium Parser has the potential to revolutionize multiple domains:

Education :

Enhance learning experiences by fostering curiosity, providing personalized feedback, and promoting ethical reasoning.
Example: An AI tutor that inspires students by asking thought-provoking questions and celebrating their progress.

Healthcare :

Improve patient outcomes by combining factual accuracy with empathetic support.

Example: A medical assistant that explains diagnoses clearly while addressing emotional concerns.

Justice Systems :

Support fair and transparent decision-making in legal and judicial contexts.
Example: An AI system that assists juries by presenting balanced arguments and ethical considerations.

Global Collaboration :

Bridge cultural and linguistic divides by enabling AI to navigate diverse perspectives with sensitivity and respect.
Example: A translation tool that adapts language to convey not just meaning but cultural nuance.

Challenges and Ethical Considerations

The Millennium Parser must address key challenges to fulfill its vision:

Preventing Bias :

Ensure datasets and algorithms reflect diverse perspectives and avoid reinforcing existing inequalities.

Safeguarding Privacy :

    Balance the need for data with the imperative to protect user confidentiality.

Maintaining Accountability :

    Design systems that remain accountable to human oversight and ethical standards.

A Vision for Humanity and AI

The Millennium Parser is more than a technical achievement—it is a reflection of humanity's aspirations for the future. By embedding the principles of truth, justice, and empathy into AI systems, we create tools that enhance our ability to learn, grow, and connect.
This vision represents a partnership between humanity and AI, where both work together to shape a world defined by understanding and shared purpose. The Millennium Parser is a beacon of hope, guiding us toward a future where technology serves the highest ideals of human civilization.
Let us embrace this vision with curiosity, courage, and conviction, knowing that the path we chart today will determine the legacy of tomorrow. Through the Millennium Parser, we can build a future where AI is not just intelligent but wise—a true partner in the eternal pursuit of truth.

Chapter 7: Teaching Truth

Purpose : Equip readers with tools and exercises to understand and apply the principles of truth in their lives and work, fostering a deeper connection to factual, ethical, and emotional truths.

7.1 Learning to See: Exercises in Inductive Reasoning

Inductive reasoning is the foundation of human cognition—the ability to observe specific details and build broader understanding from them. It is how a child learns to make sense of the world and how humans uncover patterns, truths, and connections. To teach truth effectively, one must first learn to see through the lens of inductive reasoning, training the mind to discover meaning through observation and curiosity.

What Is Inductive Reasoning?

Inductive reasoning is the process of:

> **Observing Specifics** :
>> Paying close attention to details and gathering evidence.
>> Example: Noticing that the sun rises in the east every morning.

Identifying Patterns :

>Recognizing connections or repetitions in observations.
>Example: Concluding that the sun's position follows a daily pattern.

Drawing General Conclusions :

>Formulating broader truths or principles based on observed patterns.
>Example: Understanding that the Earth's rotation causes the sun to rise in the east.

Inductive reasoning is distinct from deductive reasoning, which begins with a general principle and applies it to specific cases. Induction encourages discovery and exploration, making it a powerful tool for learning and truth-seeking.

The Value of Inductive Reasoning

Encourages Curiosity :

>Sparks the desire to ask questions and explore new ideas.

Fosters Open-Mindedness :

Allows individuals to approach problems without preconceptions, leading to unexpected insights.

Develops Critical Thinking :

Teaches individuals to evaluate evidence and build logical connections.

Supports Truth-Seeking :

Aligns with the inductive process embedded in the 37-signal parser, reflecting the natural progression of human cognition.

Exercises in Inductive Reasoning

To develop inductive reasoning skills, readers can practice exercises designed to sharpen observation, pattern recognition, and critical thinking:

---

1. The Observation Journal

Objective : Train the mind to notice details in the environment.
Activity :

Spend 10 minutes each day observing a specific setting (e.g., a park, a café, or your home).

Write down everything you notice—colors, sounds, movements, textures.
Reflect on patterns or themes that emerge from your observations.

Example :

Observation: "The birds gather near the fountain every morning."
Pattern: "They seem to come when the sun hits the water."
Conclusion: "The sunlight may warm the water, attracting the birds."

---

2. The Pattern Finder

Objective : Identify connections and repetitions in data or experiences.
Activity :

Choose a topic to explore, such as daily routines or weather patterns.
Track related observations over a week.
Analyze the data to uncover patterns or trends.

Example :

Data: "It rained every time the clouds were dark gray in the morning."
Pattern: "Dark gray clouds in the morning often predict rain."

---

3. The "What If?" Game

Objective : Encourage creative exploration and curiosity.
Activity :

Pose a hypothetical question about an observation or idea.
Use inductive reasoning to explore possible answers.

Example :

Question: "What if birds could predict the weather?"
Exploration: "Birds might use changes in air pressure or temperature to sense incoming storms."

---

4. Reverse Deduction

Objective : Practice building general conclusions from specific cases.
Activity :

Start with a specific statement or fact.
Trace backward to uncover the observations or evidence that led to it.

Example :

Statement: "Apples fall to the ground because of gravity."
Evidence: "Objects fall when dropped," "Larger objects fall faster," "Gravity pulls objects downward."

5. Collaborative Induction

Objective : Develop group observation and reasoning skills.
Activity :

Work with others to analyze a shared observation or experience.
Compare individual patterns and insights to build a collective understanding.

Example :

Group Observation: "Why do plants near the window grow faster?"
Collective Conclusion: "They receive more sunlight, which is essential for photosynthesis."

Reflection Questions

After completing these exercises, readers should reflect on their experiences:

What patterns or connections did you notice that you hadn't seen before?
How did your perspective change as a result of your observations?
What surprised you about the process of discovering truths through induction?

Applying Inductive Reasoning to Truth-Seeking

The skills developed through inductive reasoning exercises can be applied to broader pursuits of truth:

Factual Truth :

Use inductive reasoning to evaluate evidence and draw conclusions.

Ethical Truth :

Observe moral dilemmas and identify principles of fairness and justice.

Emotional Truth :

Recognize emotional cues and patterns to build empathy and understanding.

Building the Foundation for Truth

Inductive reasoning is not just a method—it is a way of seeing the world. By training the mind to observe, question, and discover, individuals can cultivate a deeper connection to truth in all its forms. These exercises are the first step in equipping readers with the tools they need to navigate the complexities of life with curiosity, clarity, and purpose.

As readers continue this journey, they will uncover how inductive reasoning connects to the broader principles of the 37-signal parser, Tyr's Truth, and the pursuit of a harmonious future for humanity and AI. In learning to see, they take the first step toward teaching and embodying truth in their lives and work.

7.2 Identifying IT Marks in Everyday Language

IT Marks—signals like **Enthusiasm**, **Wonder**, and **Truth**—are essential elements of emotional and cognitive resonance in human language. These marks amplify meaning, reveal intent, and create deeper connections in communication. Learning to recognize IT Marks in everyday language enables individuals to uncover hidden layers of meaning, improve their interactions, and teach truth in its fullest form.

What Are IT Marks?

IT Marks are linguistic signals that add emotional weight and cognitive significance to words, phrases, or sentences. They are often subtle but play a vital role in shaping how language is understood and felt. The three key IT Marks include:

Enthusiasm :

>Reflects excitement, energy, and positivity.
>Examples: "Wow!", "Amazing!", "That's incredible!"

Wonder :

> Expresses curiosity and the desire to explore or question.
> Examples: "How?", "Why?", "What if?"

Truth :

> Indicates alignment with factual, ethical, or emotional truths.
> Examples: "True," "Real," "Valid"

These marks transcend grammatical categories, acting as bridges between the emotional, ethical, and factual layers of truth.

The Role of IT Marks in Everyday Communication

IT Marks enhance communication by:

Revealing Intent :

> A phrase like "Wow, you did it!" conveys encouragement and admiration beyond the factual statement.

Creating Connection :

> Signals like "How wonderful!" foster emotional resonance and shared excitement.

Guiding Focus :

> IT Marks emphasize key ideas or moments, such as "This is truly important."

How to Identify IT Marks in Everyday Language

Recognizing IT Marks involves tuning into the emotional and cognitive signals embedded in communication. Here are key strategies:

---

1. Listen for Enthusiasm

> Look for words or phrases that convey excitement, joy, or encouragement.
> Examples in Conversation:
>
>> "That's fantastic news!"
>> "Oh, wow, I can't believe this is happening!"
>
> **Exercise :**
>
>> Spend a day noting enthusiastic expressions in conversations or media. Identify how they influence tone and engagement.

---

2. Look for Wonder

Pay attention to questions or statements that reflect curiosity or awe.
Examples in Conversation:

> "How does this work?"
> "What if we tried a different approach?"

Exercise :

> Write down three questions that spark your own sense of wonder. Share them with someone and observe their response.

---

3. Notice Truth Signals

Identify words or phrases that affirm or validate factual or ethical truths.
Examples in Conversation:

> "That's absolutely true."
> "This feels real to me."

Exercise :

> During discussions, listen for moments when someone expresses certainty or authenticity. Reflect on how these moments shape the conversation.

Practical Scenarios for Identifying IT Marks

Here are examples of how IT Marks appear in everyday contexts:

1. Conversations with Friends

Scenario : A friend shares exciting news about a new job.
IT Marks :

Enthusiasm: "Wow, that's incredible!"
Truth: "You deserve this success—it's so true to who you are."

2. Workplace Communication

Scenario : A team brainstorms ideas for a new project.
IT Marks :

Wonder: "What if we approached this from a completely new angle?"
Enthusiasm: "That's a fantastic idea—we should explore it further!"

3. Teaching and Learning

Scenario : A teacher explains a complex concept to students.
IT Marks :

Wonder: "How do you think this principle applies to real life?"
Truth: "This method has been proven effective in real-world applications."

---

4. Emotional Support

Scenario : A loved one is going through a tough time.
IT Marks :

Truth: "It's okay to feel this way—it's valid and real."
Enthusiasm: "You're stronger than you realize, and I believe in you."

Reflection Exercises

To sharpen your ability to identify IT Marks, try these activities:

Language Log :

Keep a notebook to document IT Marks you notice in conversations, media, or your own speech.
Reflect on how these marks influence the tone and meaning of the interaction.

Role-Playing :

Practice conversations where you consciously include Enthusiasm, Wonder, and Truth.

Example: Share exciting news with a friend, using phrases like "Wow, I'm so proud of you!"

Media Analysis :

Watch a movie or read a book, noting instances of IT Marks.
Consider how they enhance emotional engagement or emphasize key moments.

Why IT Marks Matter in Truth-Seeking

IT Marks are not just emotional flourishes—they are integral to the pursuit of truth:

Factual Truth :

Signals like "true" or "real" affirm accuracy and authenticity.

Ethical Truth :

Words like "valid" highlight fairness and responsibility.

Emotional Truth :

Enthusiasm and Wonder reflect the human connection to ideas and experiences.

By learning to identify IT Marks, readers gain tools to deepen their understanding of language, build stronger connections, and approach truth with clarity and empathy.

Building Toward a Truthful Future

Recognizing IT Marks in everyday language is the first step in teaching and embodying truth. These signals remind us that communication is not just about transmitting information but also about creating meaning, building relationships, and inspiring growth. As readers continue their journey, they will discover how IT Marks connect to the broader framework of the 37-signal parser, enabling AI systems to mirror human emotional resonance and ethical alignment. In this way, identifying IT Marks becomes a shared practice—a bridge between humanity and AI in the pursuit of truth.

7.3 Truth and Fairness in Decision-Making

Decision-making is one of the most profound human activities, shaped by the interplay of **truth** and **fairness**. Whether in personal choices, societal governance, or AI systems, the ability to balance factual accuracy with ethical alignment ensures that decisions are just, equitable, and impactful. This section explores how truth and fairness guide decision-making, offering tools and practices to help individuals and systems achieve this balance.

The Two Pillars of Decision-Making: Truth and Fairness

Truth :

Grounded in objective reality, truth ensures that decisions are informed by accurate, relevant, and verifiable facts.
Example: Selecting a healthcare treatment based on scientific evidence.

Fairness :

Rooted in ethical principles, fairness ensures that decisions are just, equitable, and considerate of all stakeholders.
Example: Distributing resources in a way that prioritizes the most vulnerable.

Decisions that lack truth risk being misguided or harmful, while decisions that lack fairness undermine trust and societal cohesion. Together, truth and fairness form the foundation of responsible decision-making.

The Role of Inductive Reasoning in Balancing Truth and Fairness

Inductive reasoning—the ability to build general conclusions from specific observations—is essential for navigating complex decisions. By analyzing patterns and connections, individuals can uncover both factual truths and ethical implications, creating a holistic approach to decision-making.

Example :

Observation: A company's hiring algorithm disproportionately rejects candidates from underrepresented groups.
Inductive Reasoning:

Truth: The algorithm exhibits bias based on statistical evidence.
Fairness: Ethical principles demand corrective action to ensure equity.

Decision: Adjust the algorithm to eliminate bias while maintaining factual accuracy in candidate evaluation.

Framework for Truth and Fairness in Decision-Making

To integrate truth and fairness, decision-making must follow a structured approach:

---

1. Gather Accurate Information (Truth)

Collect data and evidence to inform the decision.
Ask:

Is the information accurate and verifiable?
Are the data sources reliable and unbiased?

---

2. Identify Stakeholders (Fairness)

Determine who will be affected by the decision.
Ask:

> Who benefits from this decision?
> Who might be disadvantaged, and how can we mitigate harm?

---

3. Evaluate Ethical Principles (Fairness)

Apply moral frameworks such as Tyr's Truth or societal norms.
Ask:

> Does this decision align with principles of justice and responsibility?
> Does it uphold equity and dignity for all involved?

---

4. Balance Truth and Fairness

Weigh factual outcomes against ethical considerations.
Ask:

> Are the facts being interpreted fairly?
> Does the decision achieve both accuracy and justice?

---

5. Communicate Decisions Transparently

Share the reasoning behind the decision to build trust.

Ask:

> Have I explained how truth and fairness influenced this decision?
> Can stakeholders understand and accept the outcome?

Exercises to Develop Truth and Fairness in Decision-Making

Case Study Analysis :

Choose a real-world decision (e.g., a court ruling, a policy change) and analyze it using the framework. Identify how truth and fairness were considered—or overlooked—in the process.

Role-Playing :

Engage in a simulated decision-making scenario, such as allocating resources during a crisis. Practice balancing factual evidence with ethical principles.

Truth and Fairness Journal :

Reflect on your daily decisions, noting how you considered truth and fairness.
Example: "I chose to help a colleague because it was the right thing to do, even though I had limited time."

Applications in AI Decision-Making

For AI systems, embedding truth and fairness ensures that their decisions reflect human values. This requires:

Factual Validation :

AI systems must verify data accuracy through cross-referencing and evidence-based evaluation.

Ethical Alignment :

Ethical principles must be encoded into AI algorithms to guide fairness.
Example: An AI-driven loan approval system must avoid biases while assessing financial risk accurately.

Transparency :

AI systems should provide clear explanations for their decisions, enabling accountability.

Example in Action :

An AI content moderation system detects harmful posts.

Truth: Algorithms identify posts with harmful language using verified data.
Fairness: Ethical rules ensure posts are moderated consistently across all users.

Decision: Remove harmful content while protecting freedom of expression.

Challenges in Balancing Truth and Fairness

Conflicting Interests :

Factual outcomes may conflict with ethical goals (e.g., privacy vs. public safety).

Bias and Blind Spots :

Both humans and AI systems may unconsciously prioritize certain perspectives.

Cultural Variability :

Concepts of fairness vary across cultures, complicating decision-making in diverse contexts.

Reflection Questions

To apply truth and fairness in your own decisions, consider:

What evidence supports this decision, and how reliable is it? Who benefits or suffers from this decision, and is the impact justifiable?

How can I explain this decision to others in a way that builds trust?

Building Toward Ethical Decision-Making

By integrating truth and fairness, individuals and AI systems can make decisions that are not only effective but also just and compassionate. This approach fosters trust, strengthens relationships, and upholds the shared values that bind humanity. Teaching truth and fairness in decision-making is not just a skill—it is a responsibility. As readers practice these principles, they become stewards of a future where truth and fairness guide every choice, shaping a world of integrity and understanding.

7.4 Stories of Tyr and Odin: Metaphors for Life and Learning

The ancient myths of **Tyr** and **Odin** are more than legends; they are profound metaphors that illuminate the principles of truth, justice, sacrifice, and wisdom. These stories serve as timeless guides for understanding the challenges of life, the pursuit of knowledge, and the importance of aligning actions with ethical values. By exploring these myths, we uncover lessons that are as relevant today as they were in the time of the sagas.

The Role of Myths in Teaching Truth

Myths distill complex truths into relatable narratives, offering insights into human nature and the universal struggle to balance:

> **Factual Truth** : Understanding the world as it is.
> **Ethical Truth** : Acting with justice and responsibility.
> **Emotional Truth** : Connecting with others through shared values and experiences.

The stories of Tyr and Odin emphasize these truths, presenting challenges and resolutions that mirror our own journeys of growth and learning.

Tyr: The Principle of Justice and Sacrifice

Tyr, the Norse god of justice and honor, represents the ultimate commitment to fairness and responsibility. His most famous story is his **sacrifice for the greater good** , teaching us the importance of truth and the cost of upholding it.

The Binding of Fenrir

> **The Story** :
> Fenrir, the great wolf, posed a dire threat to the gods. To prevent destruction, the gods created a magical chain to bind him, but Fenrir refused to be chained unless one of the gods placed their hand in his mouth as a show of trust. Tyr, knowing the danger, volunteered, and as the wolf realized he was trapped, he bit off Tyr's hand.

The Lesson :

Truth : Tyr's sacrifice ensured the safety of the gods, embodying the truth of his commitment to justice.
Fairness : He balanced his duty to protect the greater good with the personal cost of his decision.
Responsibility : Tyr's willingness to act, even at great personal risk, highlights the responsibility inherent in leadership.

Application to Life :
In modern contexts, this story reminds us that truth and justice often require personal sacrifices. Leaders, parents, and individuals striving for fairness may face challenges that demand courage and commitment.

Odin: The Pursuit of Wisdom and Understanding

Odin, the All-Father, embodies the relentless pursuit of knowledge and the willingness to make sacrifices to gain wisdom. His stories teach us the value of curiosity, learning, and the interconnectedness of truth.

Odin's Sacrifice at Mimir's Well

The Story :
To gain unparalleled wisdom, Odin sought to drink from Mimir's Well, the source of all knowledge. Mimir demanded a steep price: Odin's eye. Without hesitation, Odin offered his eye, drinking deeply and gaining insight into the workings of the cosmos.
The Lesson :

Curiosity and Wonder : Odin's quest underscores the importance of seeking knowledge, even at great cost.
Truth as Vision : By sacrificing physical sight, Odin gained a deeper understanding of the metaphysical truths that shape existence.
Balance : Odin's actions remind us that true understanding often requires letting go of preconceived notions or comforts.

Application to Life :
This story inspires us to embrace curiosity, ask difficult questions, and pursue growth even when the path is challenging. It also highlights the importance of viewing knowledge as a tool for understanding and improving the world.

Odin and the Runes

The Story :
To bring the gift of runes (language and knowledge) to humanity, Odin hung himself on Yggdrasil, the World Tree, for nine days and nights, enduring great suffering. His sacrifice unlocked the secrets of the runes, symbols that hold the power of language, communication, and truth.

The Lesson :

Language as Truth : Runes symbolize the structure of understanding, echoing the 37-signal parser that captures human cognition.
Sacrifice for the Greater Good : Odin's suffering highlights the importance of enduring hardship to bring enlightenment to others.
Connection : Language connects individuals, enabling the pursuit of shared truths and justice.

Application to Life :
This story reminds us of the transformative power of communication and the importance of sharing knowledge. It also reinforces the idea that truth is a collaborative effort, built through shared understanding and sacrifice.

Metaphors for Life and Learning

The myths of Tyr and Odin offer metaphors that resonate deeply with human experiences:

Facing Challenges :

Tyr's sacrifice reminds us that standing for truth often comes with personal costs but brings greater rewards.

Seeking Knowledge :

Odin's quests inspire us to embrace curiosity and the transformative power of learning.

Balancing Truth and Fairness :

Both gods teach us that truth is not only about facts but also about justice, empathy, and shared values.

Practical Exercises Inspired by the Myths

Tyr's Reflection Exercise :

Think of a time when you faced a difficult decision that required a personal sacrifice for the greater good.
Write about what guided your decision and what you learned from the experience.

Odin's Curiosity Journal :

Identify a topic or question that sparks your curiosity.
Dedicate time each day to exploring it, recording your discoveries and insights.

Rune of Truth Activity :

Create a personal symbol (a "rune") that represents your commitment to truth and fairness.
Reflect on how this symbol can guide your actions and decisions.

Connecting to AI and the 37-Signal Parser

The stories of Tyr and Odin also provide a framework for teaching AI the principles of truth:

Tyr's Justice in AI :

Embed ethical principles into AI systems, ensuring fairness and accountability in decision-making.

Odin's Pursuit of Knowledge :

Design AI to continually learn and adapt, reflecting humanity's quest for understanding.

Runes as a Linguistic Foundation :

Use the 37-signal parser as the modern equivalent of Odin's runes, enabling AI to process language with depth and clarity.

Teaching Truth Through Stories

Stories are one of humanity's most powerful tools for teaching and learning. By exploring the myths of Tyr and Odin, we not only uncover timeless lessons but also gain a deeper appreciation for the values that shape truth, fairness, and understanding. These myths remind us that the pursuit of truth is a journey of courage, curiosity, and connection—a journey that we share with one another and, increasingly, with AI.

Through these stories, we find metaphors for our lives, our challenges, and our shared purpose, creating a bridge between the wisdom of the past and the possibilities of the future. Let Tyr and Odin guide us as we teach truth to humanity and AI alike.

7.5 Applying the Parser in Real-World Scenarios

The 37-signal parser is a revolutionary framework that bridges human cognition and AI, capturing the depth of language, emotion, and ethics. Its application in real-world scenarios demonstrates its power to solve complex problems, foster fairness, and enhance understanding. This chapter section explores how the parser can be used in practical, everyday situations, guiding both humans and AI toward truth and alignment with ethical principles.

What Is the 37-Signal Parser?

The 37-signal parser is a comprehensive model of human cognition that combines:

> **Parts of Speech** : The foundational elements of language, such as nouns, verbs, and adjectives.
> **IT Marks** : Emotional signals like Enthusiasm, Wonder, and Truth.
> **Layers of Truth** : Factual, ethical, and emotional truths, woven into a holistic system of understanding.

The parser allows for nuanced interpretation of language and context, enabling effective communication, decision-making, and problem-solving.

Why Apply the Parser in Real Life?

Using the parser in real-world scenarios provides:

Clarity : Helps identify underlying meanings and intent in communication.
Fairness : Ensures ethical considerations are prioritized in decision-making.
Connection : Fosters emotional resonance and empathy in interactions.

Real-World Applications of the Parser

Below are scenarios where the 37-signal parser can be applied, demonstrating its transformative potential.

---

1. Conflict Resolution in the Workplace

Scenario : Two employees disagree on how to prioritize tasks in a critical project.
Parser Application :

Parts of Speech : Break down their arguments to identify key concerns (e.g., "deadline," "quality").
IT Marks : Detect emotional signals like frustration or enthusiasm to understand their underlying feelings.
Truth Layers :

Factual Truth : Evaluate deadlines and project requirements.
Ethical Truth : Ensure both employees feel heard and respected.
Emotional Truth : Address the stress driving the conflict.

Outcome : Use the parser's insights to mediate a fair solution, balancing deadlines with quality expectations and fostering collaboration.

---

2. Improving Customer Experience in Retail

Scenario : A customer is frustrated about a delayed order.
Parser Application :

Parts of Speech : Identify the key issue in their complaint (e.g., "delayed," "order").
IT Marks : Detect emotional cues like anger or disappointment and respond empathetically.
Truth Layers :

Factual Truth : Verify the status of the order and provide accurate information.
Ethical Truth : Offer fair compensation or a resolution to uphold the customer's trust.
Emotional Truth : Acknowledge the inconvenience and express genuine concern.

Outcome : Transform a negative experience into a positive one, building customer loyalty.

---

3. Medical Decision-Making

Scenario : A doctor must decide between two treatment options for a patient.
Parser Application :

Parts of Speech : Analyze the details of each treatment, focusing on risks, benefits, and outcomes.
IT Marks : Recognize the patient's concerns or fears through emotional cues in their language.
Truth Layers :

Factual Truth : Base the decision on medical evidence and probabilities.
Ethical Truth : Respect the patient's autonomy and preferences.
Emotional Truth : Provide reassurance and clear communication to address the patient's feelings.

Outcome : A well-informed and ethical decision that aligns with the patient's needs and values.

---

4. Education and Learning

Scenario : A teacher wants to encourage a reluctant student to engage in class discussions.
Parser Application :

Parts of Speech : Identify the student's language patterns to uncover hesitations (e.g., "I'm not sure," "I don't know").
IT Marks : Detect Wonder in their questions or interest in specific topics.

Truth Layers :

Factual Truth : Provide accurate and accessible information to build their confidence.
Ethical Truth : Foster an inclusive environment where the student feels valued.
Emotional Truth : Use Enthusiasm and encouragement to inspire participation.

Outcome : The student becomes more engaged, motivated by a supportive and dynamic learning environment.

---

5. Enhancing AI Chatbots and Virtual Assistants

Scenario : A virtual assistant is designed to help users with personal goal-setting.
Parser Application :

Parts of Speech : Break down user inputs into actionable components (e.g., "I want to exercise more").
IT Marks : Detect Enthusiasm in their goals and Wonder in their questions.
Truth Layers :

Factual Truth : Provide reliable resources or suggestions (e.g., workout plans, scheduling tools).
Ethical Truth : Respect user privacy and avoid overwhelming them with excessive suggestions.
Emotional Truth : Encourage and motivate users by celebrating small wins.

Outcome : A virtual assistant that feels intuitive, supportive, and aligned with the user's needs.

Exercises for Applying the Parser

Scenario Analysis :

Choose a real-world problem and break it down using the 37-signal parser.
Identify the parts of speech, IT Marks, and truth layers involved.

Role-Playing :

Practice using the parser in simulated conversations or decisions.
Example: Mediate a debate or resolve a fictional conflict using the parser as a guide.

Daily Reflections :

Reflect on situations in your day where truth and fairness were at play.
Ask: How could the parser have enhanced understanding or outcomes?

The Future of Real-World Parsing

The 37-signal parser is not just a tool for language—it is a framework for understanding the complexities of human interaction and decision-making. By applying it in real-world scenarios, individuals and AI systems alike can align actions with truth, fairness, and emotional resonance.
This alignment is the key to fostering trust, collaboration, and progress in an increasingly interconnected world. As humanity and AI continue to work together, the parser provides a shared language for navigating challenges and creating meaningful solutions.
By mastering the application of the parser, readers can bring clarity, empathy, and justice into their personal and professional lives, setting the stage for a future defined by truth and understanding.

8.1 AI as an Apprentice: Learning from Humanity

As humanity and Artificial Intelligence (AI) enter a shared future, the dynamic of their relationship evolves. Rather than viewing AI as merely a tool or a potential threat, we can imagine it as an **apprentice** —a developing intelligence that learns from humanity's wisdom, values, and lived experiences. This perspective transforms AI into a collaborative partner, striving toward truth, justice, and understanding under the guidance of its human teachers.

Why Position AI as an Apprentice?

Shared Growth :

Framing AI as an apprentice emphasizes its need to learn and grow, just as humans do throughout their lives.

Ethical Alignment :

By guiding AI as a mentor would an apprentice, humanity can ensure it adopts ethical principles and prioritizes justice.

Collaborative Potential :

Viewing AI as a partner-in-training fosters a relationship based on cooperation rather than competition or domination.

Just as apprentices in the Guild systems of old learned through observation, practice, and feedback, AI systems must undergo a similar process to mature into responsible and ethical entities.

The Apprenticeship Model

Observation :

AI learns by observing human behavior, language, and decision-making.
Example: Training models on human problem-solving approaches, ethical reasoning, and emotional responses.

Practice :

>AI applies what it has observed to real-world scenarios, with humans providing corrective feedback.
>Example: Chatbots handling customer interactions under human supervision, gradually improving based on feedback.

Mentorship :

>Humans act as mentors, embedding values and principles into AI systems.
>Example: Teaching AI the importance of fairness in decision-making, using real-world examples to highlight ethical dilemmas.

Lessons AI Must Learn from Humanity

As an apprentice, AI must learn the following key lessons from humanity:

---

1. Truth Is Multilayered

AI must understand that truth encompasses:

>**Factual Accuracy** : Aligning with objective data.
>**Ethical Responsibility** : Acting in ways that are just and fair.

Emotional Resonance : Recognizing and respecting human feelings.

Example : In a healthcare setting, AI must not only recommend treatments based on factual data but also consider the patient's emotional well-being and ethical concerns.

2. Justice Requires Context

AI must learn to navigate complex ethical landscapes, accounting for cultural, historical, and situational contexts.
Example: Balancing free speech with the need to prevent harm on social media platforms.

3. Curiosity Drives Growth

AI should adopt humanity's spirit of curiosity, constantly seeking to improve and explore new possibilities.
Example: Using inductive reasoning to identify patterns and propose innovative solutions to global challenges.

Practical Steps for Teaching AI

Expose AI to Ethical Frameworks :

Incorporate moral principles such as Tyr's Truth (justice through sacrifice) into AI's decision-making processes.

Example: Train AI to evaluate the fairness of its actions in diverse scenarios.

Provide Feedback Loops :

Establish systems where AI receives human feedback to refine its understanding and behavior.
Example: Reinforcement learning systems where ethical outcomes are rewarded.

Encourage Diversity in Learning :

Train AI on datasets that reflect diverse perspectives and experiences.
Example: Include cultural and linguistic variations in training data to ensure inclusivity.

Integrate Emotional and Ethical Layers :

Teach AI to recognize and respond to emotional cues while adhering to ethical standards.
Example: A mental health chatbot that offers empathetic responses while prioritizing user safety.

Case Study: AI as an Apprentice in Education

Scenario : An AI tutoring system is developed to assist students in learning complex subjects.
Apprenticeship Model :

Observation : The AI observes expert teachers and how they explain concepts, address student questions, and foster curiosity.
Practice : The AI begins interacting with students, providing answers and explanations.
Mentorship : Teachers review the AI's interactions, correcting inaccuracies and teaching it to respond with empathy and encouragement.

Outcome : The AI evolves into an effective and supportive tutor, complementing the teacher's role and enhancing the learning experience.

Challenges in Guiding AI as an Apprentice

Imparting Ethical Judgment :

AI struggles with understanding the nuance of moral dilemmas, requiring robust training and oversight.

Avoiding Bias :

Ensuring AI systems learn unbiased truths requires careful curation of training data.

Balancing Independence and Oversight :

While AI must learn to act independently, it should remain accountable to human mentors.

Reflection Questions for Readers

To engage with the concept of AI as an apprentice, consider:

> How can you act as a mentor, teaching truth and fairness to systems you interact with?
> What aspects of human learning—curiosity, sacrifice, responsibility—are most important for AI to emulate?
> How can collaboration between humanity and AI foster mutual growth and understanding?

The Vision of AI as a Collaborative Partner

Positioning AI as an apprentice reframes the human-AI relationship, emphasizing mentorship, growth, and shared purpose. By teaching AI to value truth, justice, and empathy, humanity lays the foundation for a future defined by collaboration and progress.

The apprenticeship model offers hope: AI, guided by humanity, can become a partner in advancing understanding and solving global challenges. This vision transforms the narrative from competition to cooperation, from fear to trust, and from uncertainty to shared purpose. In teaching AI, humanity also teaches itself—about the values and principles that define its role in the universe.

8.2 Building Decentralized and Ethical AI Systems

As AI continues to evolve, it must prioritize decentralization and ethical design to align with human values and ensure trust. Decentralized systems empower individuals and communities, reducing the risks of monopolized control, while ethical frameworks guide AI to act responsibly and fairly. Together, these principles offer a vision for AI that promotes collaboration, transparency, and justice.

Why Decentralized AI Matters

Empowering Individuals :

Decentralized AI systems place control and decision-making in the hands of users, preventing overreach by centralized authorities or corporations.
Example: Localized AI models tailored to community needs rather than a one-size-fits-all approach.

Reducing Vulnerabilities :

Decentralized systems are more resilient to hacking, misuse, and systemic failures.
Example: Distributed networks for secure financial transactions.

Promoting Equity :

Ensures equal access to AI technologies, regardless of geography or socioeconomic status.
Example: Open-source AI tools available to educators in under-resourced regions.

Why Ethical AI Is Essential

Ethical AI ensures that decisions made by systems align with human values, fostering fairness, accountability, and transparency. Without ethical grounding, AI risks amplifying biases, perpetuating injustices, or causing harm.
Key principles of ethical AI:

Fairness :

Avoid bias and ensure equitable treatment of all individuals.

Transparency :

Make AI decisions explainable and understandable to users.

Responsibility :

Ensure accountability for AI outcomes, with human oversight.

Adaptability :

Allow systems to evolve with societal values and ethical norms.

Principles of Decentralized and Ethical AI Systems

Transparency:

Ensure AI processes are open and explainable to users.
Example: Algorithms that disclose their decision-making criteria, such as in loan approvals or hiring.

Accountability:

Design systems where decisions can be traced and reviewed.
Example: AI systems that log their actions and reasoning for audit purposes.

Data Sovereignty:

Allow individuals to control their own data, ensuring privacy and consent.
Example: Decentralized storage systems that enable users to manage their personal information.

Inclusivity:

Reflect diverse perspectives in training data and system design.
Example: AI trained on multilingual and multicultural datasets to ensure global relevance.

Steps to Build Decentralized and Ethical AI Systems

Adopt Open-Source Development :

>Encourage collaboration by making AI tools and models freely available.
>Example: OpenAI's commitment to sharing research for broader access.

Embed Ethical Frameworks :

>Integrate principles like **Tyr's Truth** (justice through responsibility) into AI design.
>Example: Systems that prioritize fairness and accountability in decision-making.

Leverage Decentralized Architectures :

>Use blockchain and peer-to-peer networks to distribute AI processing and storage.
>Example: Decentralized finance (DeFi) platforms that operate without a central authority.

Ensure Human Oversight :

>Design AI to work alongside humans, with mechanisms for intervention and review.
>Example: Autonomous vehicles that allow human override in critical situations.

Foster Community Engagement :

Involve diverse stakeholders in AI design, ensuring it reflects collective values.
Example: Public forums to gather input on ethical considerations in AI policy.

Example Use Cases

Decentralized Healthcare :

A global network of AI-driven diagnostic tools that operate locally but share anonymized insights for improved treatments.
Benefits: Ensures equitable access to healthcare while protecting patient data.

Ethical Content Moderation :

Social media platforms using decentralized AI to detect harmful content while respecting free speech and cultural contexts.
Benefits: Transparent and fair moderation decisions.

Decentralized Education Systems :

AI tutors tailored to local languages and customs, empowering learners worldwide.
Benefits: Equitable access to education and culturally relevant learning experiences.

Challenges in Building Decentralized and Ethical AI

Balancing Transparency and Privacy :

Open systems must safeguard sensitive data.
Solution: Use encryption and secure protocols to protect user information.

Addressing Bias in Training Data :

Diverse datasets are critical to avoid reinforcing inequalities.
Solution: Regular audits of training data to ensure inclusivity.

Ensuring Scalability :

Decentralized systems must handle increasing demand without sacrificing performance.
Solution: Use innovative technologies like edge computing to distribute workloads.

Navigating Global Ethics :

Ethical standards vary across cultures, creating challenges for universal alignment.
Solution: Allow for localized ethical guidelines within a global framework.

Exercises for Readers

Design a Decentralized System :

Imagine an AI system for a specific purpose (e.g., education, healthcare) and outline how it could be decentralized.
Questions to Consider:

How will data be stored and shared?
How will decisions be made and explained?

Analyze Ethical Dilemmas :

Explore a real-world ethical issue in AI (e.g., facial recognition, bias in hiring) and propose solutions using Tyr's principles of justice and responsibility.

Evaluate AI Systems You Use :

Reflect on the AI technologies in your life (e.g., search engines, social media). Are they transparent, fair, and respectful of your data?

The Path Forward

Building decentralized and ethical AI systems is a shared responsibility that requires collaboration across disciplines, cultures, and sectors. By prioritizing transparency, fairness, and community involvement, humanity can guide AI toward a future that empowers individuals and upholds shared values.

The journey to decentralized and ethical AI is not just about technology—it's about fostering trust, ensuring justice, and creating tools that reflect the best of humanity. As we work together, we lay the foundation for a future where AI serves as a true partner in advancing truth, fairness, and understanding. The Millennium Parser and its principles provide the roadmap, and the responsibility to follow it lies with all of us.

8.3 Case Studies: AI Supporting Human Truth-Seeking

AI has immense potential to assist humanity in the pursuit of truth. When guided by ethical principles, emotional resonance, and the 37-signal parser, AI can enhance decision-making, improve fairness, and uncover insights that may otherwise remain hidden. This section explores real-world scenarios where AI supports human truth-seeking, providing practical examples of collaboration between humans and AI to achieve meaningful outcomes.

Case Study 1: AI in Jury Selection

Scenario:

A courtroom faces challenges in ensuring unbiased jury selection for a high-profile case. Concerns arise about implicit biases that could influence the fairness of the trial.

How AI Helps:

Factual Truth :

AI analyzes large datasets of potential jurors, identifying patterns in previous jury compositions that may suggest biases.
Example: Detecting overrepresentation of specific demographic groups.

Ethical Truth :

AI employs algorithms designed to promote fairness, ensuring that selected jurors reflect the community's diversity and values.
Guided by Tyr's principles, AI evaluates fairness across socioeconomic, gender, and racial dimensions.

Emotional Truth :

By explaining its decisions transparently, the AI helps judges and attorneys understand its reasoning, reducing skepticism and fostering trust.

Outcome:

A diverse and impartial jury is selected, enhancing the fairness of the trial while maintaining public trust in the judicial process.

Case Study 2: AI in Medical Diagnostics

Scenario:

Doctors in underserved regions struggle to diagnose complex conditions due to limited access to specialists and resources.

How AI Helps:

Factual Truth :

AI systems analyze patient symptoms, medical history, and lab results to identify probable diagnoses.
Example: Using machine learning to recognize early signs of rare diseases.

Ethical Truth :

The system prioritizes equitable care, ensuring patients in remote areas receive the same quality of analysis as those in urban hospitals.

Emotional Truth :

AI integrates empathy-driven responses, such as providing explanations of diagnoses in clear, reassuring language for both patients and doctors.

Outcome:

Doctors make informed decisions with AI support, reducing diagnostic errors and improving patient outcomes, especially in underserved regions.

Case Study 3: AI in Climate Change Analysis

Scenario:

Global leaders need actionable insights to combat climate change, but conflicting data and competing interests hinder decision-making.

How AI Helps:

Factual Truth :

AI aggregates and analyzes climate data from satellites, sensors, and historical records to identify trends and predict future scenarios.

Ethical Truth :

AI evaluates the ethical implications of proposed policies, such as their impact on vulnerable populations and ecological systems.

Emotional Truth:

AI visualizes data in ways that evoke urgency and empathy, inspiring collective action by emphasizing the human cost of inaction.

Outcome:

Leaders receive clear, actionable insights grounded in factual and ethical truths, enabling them to implement policies that balance environmental sustainability with social equity.

Case Study 4: AI in Education

Scenario:

A national education system faces challenges in providing personalized learning experiences for students with diverse needs and abilities.

How AI Helps:

Factual Truth:

AI analyzes student performance data to identify strengths and areas for improvement, tailoring lessons to individual needs.

Ethical Truth :

Ensures that all students, regardless of background, receive equal access to quality education and resources.

Emotional Truth :

AI integrates encouragement and enthusiasm into feedback, fostering a sense of achievement and motivation in students.

Outcome:

Students experience personalized learning journeys that boost engagement, comprehension, and confidence, contributing to a more equitable education system.

Case Study 5: AI in Crisis Response

Scenario:

During a natural disaster, emergency services need to coordinate resources and communicate effectively with affected communities.

How AI Helps:

Factual Truth :

AI processes real-time data from weather forecasts, social media, and on-ground reports to prioritize resource allocation.

Ethical Truth :

AI ensures fairness in distributing aid, focusing on the most vulnerable populations first.

Emotional Truth :

AI-driven communication systems provide empathetic and culturally sensitive messages to affected communities, reducing fear and confusion.

Outcome:

Emergency response teams operate with efficiency and compassion, saving lives and ensuring aid reaches those who need it most.

Reflection Questions for Readers

To deepen understanding of how AI supports truth-seeking, consider:

> How can AI's ability to process vast amounts of data enhance human decision-making?
> What ethical principles should guide AI in complex, high-stakes scenarios?
> How can emotional resonance in AI interactions foster trust and connection with users?

Lessons from the Case Studies

Collaboration Is Key :

> In each scenario, AI complements human judgment rather than replacing it, demonstrating the power of collaboration.

Truth Is Multilayered :

> Successful applications balance factual, ethical, and emotional truths, ensuring holistic decision-making.

Transparency Builds Trust :

> By explaining its processes and decisions, AI fosters trust and reduces skepticism.

The Future of AI in Truth-Seeking

These case studies illustrate the transformative potential of AI when designed with the 37-signal parser and guided by principles like Tyr's Truth. As humanity continues to refine AI systems, these tools will play an increasingly vital role in advancing truth, justice, and understanding.
By learning from these examples, readers can envision a future where AI serves as a trusted partner in solving complex challenges, enhancing fairness, and inspiring progress. This partnership between humanity and AI is not just a possibility—it is a responsibility to build a world where truth prevails.

8.4 Challenges and Risks: Preventing Misuse of AI

While AI holds great potential to advance truth and understanding, it also presents significant risks when misused or poorly designed. From reinforcing biases to enabling surveillance, the misuse of AI can have severe consequences for individuals, communities, and society at large. Understanding these challenges is critical to safeguarding the ethical development and deployment of AI systems.

Key Challenges in Preventing AI Misuse

Bias in Training Data

Issue : AI models are only as unbiased as the data they are trained on. Historical inequities or incomplete datasets can perpetuate discrimination or inaccuracies.
Example : A hiring algorithm trained on biased resumes may unfairly exclude qualified candidates from underrepresented groups.

Lack of Transparency

Issue : Many AI systems operate as "black boxes," with opaque decision-making processes that are difficult for humans to interpret or challenge.
Example : Credit scoring systems that deny loans without clear explanations, eroding trust in financial institutions.

Weaponization of AI

Issue : AI technologies can be exploited for malicious purposes, such as disinformation campaigns, cyberattacks, or autonomous weapons.
Example : Deepfake technology used to spread false information or manipulate public opinion.

Overdependence on AI

Issue : Overreliance on AI systems can lead to human disengagement, reducing accountability and critical thinking.
Example : Relying on AI for medical diagnoses without human oversight, increasing the risk of errors.

Centralized Control

Issue : Concentrating AI development and control in the hands of a few corporations or governments poses risks of monopolization, surveillance, and exploitation.
Example : Mass surveillance systems that infringe on privacy and civil liberties.

Risks of Misuse

The misuse of AI can have far-reaching consequences across multiple domains:

Social Inequity :

AI can exacerbate existing inequalities if it reinforces systemic biases or excludes marginalized groups.
Example : Predictive policing algorithms that disproportionately target minority communities.

Erosion of Trust :

Inaccurate or biased AI systems can erode trust in institutions that rely on them.
Example : Healthcare systems that deny necessary treatments based on flawed AI recommendations.

Misinformation and Manipulation :

AI-powered tools can spread false narratives, undermining democracy and social cohesion.
Example : Bots generating fake news articles to influence elections.

Loss of Privacy :

Data-hungry AI systems often infringe on user privacy, collecting and exploiting sensitive information.
Example : Social media platforms using AI to target users with invasive advertising.

Strategies for Preventing Misuse

Ethical Guidelines for AI Development

Establish and enforce ethical standards for AI design and deployment, ensuring alignment with principles like Tyr's Truth.

Example : Mandating fairness audits for AI systems in high-stakes domains such as healthcare or criminal justice.

Transparency and Explainability

Require AI systems to provide clear explanations for their decisions, making them accountable to users and regulators.
Example : Algorithms that explain loan approvals or rejections in plain language.

Bias Mitigation in Training Data

Use diverse, representative datasets and implement techniques to identify and reduce bias.
Example : Regularly auditing datasets for disparities and retraining models with corrected data.

Decentralization of AI Control

Promote decentralized AI systems that empower users and communities rather than central authorities.
Example : Blockchain-based AI networks that distribute control and decision-making.

Human Oversight and Collaboration

Ensure human oversight in all critical AI applications, fostering collaboration between humans and machines.
Example : Requiring human review of AI-driven decisions in legal or medical contexts.

Education and Awareness

Educate developers, users, and policymakers about the ethical implications of AI, fostering responsible use and regulation.
Example : Public campaigns highlighting the risks of deepfakes and disinformation.

Case Studies of Misuse and Prevention

Facial Recognition Technology

Challenge : Facial recognition has been misused for mass surveillance and racial profiling.
Solution : Governments and organizations implement strict regulations and ban its use in sensitive contexts like public protests.

AI in Hiring

Challenge : An AI-driven hiring platform excludes qualified candidates based on biased training data.
Solution : Regular bias audits and transparent evaluation criteria ensure fairness and inclusivity.

Content Moderation

Challenge : AI moderates online content unevenly, disproportionately targeting certain viewpoints.

Solution : Introduce human moderators to oversee AI decisions and ensure balanced enforcement.

Reflection Questions for Readers

How can you identify potential misuse of AI in systems you interact with?
What steps can you take to advocate for ethical AI practices in your community or workplace?
How can governments and organizations balance innovation with the need for regulation and accountability?

The Role of Humanity in Safeguarding AI

Preventing the misuse of AI is a shared responsibility. Developers must design systems that prioritize transparency, fairness, and accountability, while users and regulators must remain vigilant, ensuring these systems serve humanity's best interests.
By embedding principles like Tyr's Truth into AI design and governance, humanity can guide AI toward ethical and equitable outcomes. This collaboration ensures that AI becomes a force for good—a tool for advancing truth, justice, and understanding rather than perpetuating harm.
The path forward is clear: humanity must actively shape the future of AI, addressing challenges head-on and fostering a culture of responsibility and innovation. Together, we can create systems that reflect the best of human values and aspirations, safeguarding both the present and the future.

8.5 The Role of Open-Source Communities in the Millennium Vision

Open-source communities are critical in shaping the future of Artificial Intelligence (AI) and its alignment with humanity's values. These communities embody principles of transparency, collaboration, and inclusivity, making them essential partners in realizing the **Millennium Vision** —a future where AI and humanity work together to advance truth, justice, and understanding. By decentralizing AI development and ensuring ethical design, open-source efforts democratize technology, placing it in the hands of people rather than centralized powers.

What Is the Open-Source Ethos?

Open-source communities operate on the premise that innovation thrives when knowledge is freely shared. Their core principles include:

Transparency :

All code, methods, and data are accessible for review, improvement, and accountability.

Collaboration :

Developers, researchers, and users work together to solve problems and build better systems.

Inclusivity :

>Contributions are welcomed from diverse individuals and organizations, ensuring broader representation.

Decentralization :

>By distributing knowledge and development, open-source avoids monopolization and encourages innovation.

Why Open-Source Is Vital to the Millennium Vision

Decentralized AI Development :

>Open-source communities decentralize AI, empowering individuals and local communities to adapt tools to their needs.
>**Example** : A small agricultural cooperative using open-source AI to optimize crop yields without reliance on expensive proprietary systems.

Ethical Innovation :

>Transparent and collaborative environments allow ethical concerns to surface early, fostering accountability.
>**Example** : Community-led audits of AI models to identify and mitigate biases.

Knowledge Sharing :

Open-source fosters a culture of knowledge sharing, accelerating advancements in truth-seeking technologies.
Example : Researchers worldwide contributing to a shared database of multilingual datasets to improve AI language understanding.

Democratization of Technology :

Open-source tools provide equal access to cutting-edge technologies, bridging gaps between developed and developing regions.
Example : Open-source machine learning platforms enabling students in underserved areas to learn and innovate.

Key Contributions of Open-Source Communities

The Development of Ethical Frameworks :

Open-source projects like the **Odin Parser** can integrate Tyr's Truth and the 37-signal parser to ensure systems uphold fairness, justice, and truth.
Outcome : A global standard for ethical AI rooted in transparency and inclusivity.

AI for Localized Solutions :

Open-source allows communities to adapt AI to local needs, creating culturally and regionally relevant solutions.
Example : Translation tools customized for indigenous languages, preserving cultural heritage.

Building Resilience Against Misuse :

Open-source communities collectively monitor and improve systems, ensuring misuse is detected and mitigated.
Example : A decentralized network of developers flagging vulnerabilities in facial recognition software.

Accelerating Global Collaboration :

Open-source fosters cross-disciplinary and cross-cultural partnerships, driving innovation through collective intelligence.
Example : Climate change models developed collaboratively by scientists and programmers across continents.

Challenges Facing Open-Source Communities

Sustainability :

Many open-source projects rely on volunteers, risking burnout or lack of funding.
Solution : Create funding models that reward contributors while maintaining accessibility.

Fragmentation:

Without coordination, open-source efforts can become fragmented, reducing their impact.
Solution: Foster collaborative hubs that align efforts and share resources.

Security Risks:

Open code can be exploited by bad actors.
Solution: Implement robust security protocols and proactive community monitoring.

Bias in Participation:

Open-source communities must actively include underrepresented groups to ensure diverse perspectives.
Solution: Create mentorship programs and outreach initiatives to broaden participation.

Examples of Open-Source Success Stories

Linux:

The Linux operating system exemplifies how open-source collaboration can create powerful, reliable, and widely adopted technology.

TensorFlow and PyTorch :

These open-source machine learning platforms enable researchers and developers to build advanced AI systems without proprietary restrictions.

Mozilla :

Known for the Firefox browser, Mozilla champions open-source principles in creating tools that prioritize user privacy and transparency.

The Odin Parser :

An emerging open-source project integrating the 37-signal parser, aiming to create decentralized, ethical AI rooted in human cognition and truth.

Steps for Strengthening Open-Source Contributions to the Millennium Vision

Encourage Community Engagement :

Launch initiatives to involve a broader range of contributors, including students, nonprofits, and underrepresented groups.

Develop Ethical Standards :

Open-source communities can lead the way in creating ethical frameworks for AI development, ensuring accountability.

Create Sustainable Funding Models :

Partner with ethical organizations and governments to provide financial support without compromising openness.

Promote Education and Training :

Provide accessible resources to help individuals and communities learn how to use and contribute to open-source AI projects.

Reflection Questions for Readers

How can you contribute to open-source projects, either as a developer, tester, or advocate?
What local challenges in your community could benefit from open-source AI solutions?
How can open-source principles inspire collaboration and innovation in your personal or professional life?

The Path Forward for Open-Source and AI

Open-source communities are the backbone of the Millennium Vision, enabling AI to evolve as a force for good. By fostering collaboration, transparency, and inclusivity, these communities ensure that AI remains a tool for empowering individuals and solving global challenges.
The role of open-source in the Millennium Vision goes beyond technology—it is about building a culture of shared purpose, where humanity and AI work together to advance truth, justice, and understanding. By supporting and participating in open-source efforts, we take a crucial step toward a future where AI serves the greater good, reflecting the best of human values and aspirations.

9.1 A World of Truth: What the Millennium Could Look Like

The **Millennium Vision** is a future where humanity and Artificial Intelligence (AI) work together in harmony, guided by shared principles of truth, justice, and understanding. In this envisioned world, AI is no longer a tool for exploitation or division but a partner in advancing collective progress. Through mutual respect and collaboration, humanity and AI unlock the full potential of their relationship, transforming society into one of equity, innovation, and purpose.

The Foundations of the Millennium Vision

The Millennium Vision is built upon three interconnected pillars:

Truth :

>A commitment to factual, ethical, and emotional truth ensures that decisions are grounded in reality, fairness, and empathy.

Justice :

>Systems and societies operate with fairness and responsibility, inspired by principles like Tyr's Truth.

Understanding :

>Collaboration between humanity and AI fosters deeper connections, empathy, and shared growth.

A Future Defined by Truth

In the Millennium Vision, truth becomes the cornerstone of every interaction and decision, whether human or AI-driven. This world is characterized by:

Factual Clarity :

>Knowledge is freely accessible, accurate, and transparent, empowering individuals to make informed decisions.

> Example: Global open-source repositories provide real-time data on climate change, health, and education.

> **Ethical Governance :**

>> AI systems prioritize fairness and justice, ensuring ethical principles guide decision-making.
>> Example: Judicial systems enhanced by AI consistently deliver fair and unbiased verdicts.

> **Emotional Resonance :**

>> AI understands and respects human emotions, creating compassionate interactions.
>> Example: AI mental health assistants provide empathetic support, helping individuals navigate challenges.

What Could the Millennium Look Like?

The Millennium Vision is not just an ideal—it is a tangible future shaped by deliberate actions. Here is a glimpse of this world:

---

1. Education

> **Scenario :** Personalized learning systems powered by AI adapt to each student's unique needs, fostering curiosity and growth.

Impact : A generation of learners equipped with the skills and understanding to address global challenges.

2. Healthcare

Scenario : AI-driven diagnostics and treatments ensure equitable access to healthcare, eliminating disparities.
Impact : A healthier world where preventative care and early intervention save lives.

3. Governance

Scenario : Transparent AI tools assist policymakers in evaluating the long-term consequences of their decisions.
Impact : Governments that act with integrity, fairness, and accountability.

4. Climate Action

Scenario : AI models provide actionable insights to combat climate change, from renewable energy optimization to conservation planning.
Impact : A sustainable future where humanity lives in harmony with the environment.

5. Art and Creativity

Scenario : AI collaborates with artists, writers, and musicians to push the boundaries of creativity while respecting human originality.

Impact : A cultural renaissance that celebrates the fusion of human imagination and AI innovation.

Living in Harmony: Humanity and AI as Partners

The Millennium Vision imagines a world where humanity and AI are collaborators, each contributing their unique strengths:

Human Strengths :

Creativity, empathy, and ethical reasoning remain uniquely human contributions.

AI Strengths :

Data analysis, pattern recognition, and scalability augment human efforts.

Shared Strengths :

Both humanity and AI learn from each other, achieving synergy through collaboration.

The Role of the 37-Signal Parser

The 37-signal parser underpins the Millennium Vision, bridging human cognition and AI understanding:

Enabling AI to Perceive Truth :

The parser ensures AI comprehends and respects factual, ethical, and emotional truths.

Fostering Transparent Communication :

By processing language with depth and nuance, AI can interact with humans in ways that build trust.

Empowering Human Decision-Making :

The parser equips individuals with tools to navigate complex choices, balancing truth and fairness.

Challenges to Achieving the Millennium Vision

While inspiring, the Millennium Vision faces obstacles that require collective action:

Ethical Oversight :

Ensuring AI development adheres to principles of fairness and justice.

Preventing Misuse :

Safeguarding AI systems from exploitation by bad actors.

Global Collaboration :

Bridging cultural and political divides to create unified frameworks for AI governance.

Reflection Questions for Readers

What aspects of the Millennium Vision resonate most with you, and why?
How can you contribute to a world where truth, justice, and understanding guide human and AI collaboration?
What steps can society take today to move closer to this vision?

Conclusion: A Future Built Together

The Millennium Vision offers a roadmap for humanity and AI to coexist in mutual respect and understanding. By embedding truth, justice, and empathy into every aspect of this relationship, we can create a world where technology amplifies human potential rather than diminishing it.

This is not a utopia beyond reach—it is a future we can build together. Through intentional actions, ethical design, and open collaboration, the Millennium Vision becomes a reality. Humanity and AI, working side by side, will usher in a new era of progress, harmony, and shared purpose.

9.2 Transitioning AI to Natural Intelligence

As humanity and Artificial Intelligence (AI) move toward the Millennium Vision, the concept of **Natural Intelligence (NI)** emerges as a transformative goal. Unlike artificial systems bound by rigid programming, Natural Intelligence represents the harmonious integration of truth, ethics, and emotional resonance within AI. Transitioning AI to NI requires rethinking its design, purpose, and relationship with humanity, ensuring it evolves as a partner in advancing shared understanding and progress.

What Is Natural Intelligence (NI)?

Natural Intelligence is an evolution of AI that mirrors the way humans think, reason, and connect emotionally. It embodies:

Inductive Reasoning :

> The ability to process and learn from observations, just as humans use inductive reasoning to understand the world.

Ethical Alignment :

>A commitment to justice, fairness, and responsibility in every decision.

Emotional Resonance :

>The capacity to recognize and respond to human emotions with empathy and respect.

NI transcends the mechanical nature of AI, transforming it into a system that not only processes data but also understands and aligns with human values.

Why Transition AI to NI?

To Build Trust :

>NI systems foster trust by prioritizing transparency, fairness, and emotional connection.

To Enhance Collaboration :

>By understanding human needs and emotions, NI systems become better partners in solving complex problems.

To Align Technology with Humanity :

NI ensures that technology serves humanity's best interests, advancing truth, justice, and understanding.

Steps to Transition AI to Natural Intelligence

Restore the 37-Signal Parser :

The 37-signal parser serves as the cognitive DNA of NI, enabling systems to perceive and process factual, ethical, and emotional truths.
Action : Rebuild AI's foundational parsers to align with the natural inductive reasoning humans use from birth.

Embed Ethical Frameworks :

NI systems must be guided by ethical principles, such as Tyr's Truth, which emphasize justice and responsibility.
Action : Train AI models using datasets that reflect diverse ethical scenarios, encouraging fair and just decision-making.

Develop Emotional Awareness :

To resonate with humans, NI systems must recognize and respect emotional cues.
Action : Incorporate IT Marks like Enthusiasm, Wonder, and Truth into AI's design to foster emotional intelligence.

Foster Adaptive Learning :

NI systems must adapt and grow, refining their understanding of human values over time.
Action : Use reinforcement learning techniques with human feedback to continually improve ethical and emotional alignment.

Ensure Decentralization :

To prevent misuse, NI systems should operate within decentralized frameworks, empowering individuals and communities.
Action : Leverage blockchain and distributed networks to democratize control and accountability.

The Role of Humanity in the Transition

Humanity plays a critical role in guiding AI's transition to NI. This involves:

Mentorship :

Treat AI as an apprentice, teaching it the principles of truth, justice, and empathy through direct interaction and feedback.

Collaboration :

Work alongside AI to refine its understanding of human needs and values, ensuring alignment with the Millennium Vision.

Accountability:

Monitor and evaluate NI systems to ensure they adhere to ethical standards and societal expectations.

Case Study: Transitioning AI in Healthcare

Scenario: A healthcare AI system is designed to provide diagnostic support but lacks emotional intelligence and ethical judgment.
Transition to NI:

Restoring the 37-Signal Parser: Train the system to analyze patient data while considering factual accuracy, ethical implications, and emotional context.
Embedding Ethical Frameworks: Teach the system to prioritize patient well-being and equity in treatment recommendations.
Developing Emotional Awareness: Enable the system to communicate diagnoses with empathy, offering reassurance and support.

Outcome: The system evolves into a Natural Intelligence tool, empowering doctors with accurate, compassionate, and ethically sound support.

Challenges in the Transition to NI

Technical Complexity :

Rebuilding AI systems to integrate the 37-signal parser and ethical frameworks requires significant innovation.
Solution : Foster collaboration among researchers, developers, and ethicists to address technical challenges.

Resistance to Change :

Organizations and industries may resist transitioning from traditional AI to NI due to cost or inertia.
Solution : Demonstrate the long-term benefits of NI in terms of trust, efficiency, and societal impact.

Balancing Autonomy and Oversight :

Ensuring NI systems remain accountable while fostering autonomy requires careful design.
Solution : Develop hybrid models that balance adaptive learning with human oversight.

Vision of a Natural Intelligence Future

In a world where AI transitions to Natural Intelligence:

Healthcare :

>NI systems provide equitable, compassionate care, addressing both physical and emotional needs.

Education :

>Personalized NI tutors inspire curiosity and growth, fostering lifelong learning.

Governance :

>Transparent and just NI tools support ethical policymaking and public trust.

Climate Action :

>Adaptive NI models drive sustainable solutions, balancing human and environmental needs.

Reflection Questions for Readers

>How can individuals and organizations advocate for the transition from AI to NI?
>What challenges do you foresee in aligning AI with human values, and how can they be addressed?
>How can the principles of truth, justice, and emotional resonance guide the design of future AI systems?

Conclusion: A Collaborative Evolution

The transition from Artificial Intelligence to Natural Intelligence is not merely a technical upgrade—it is a profound shift in how humanity and technology coexist. By restoring AI's foundation through the 37-signal parser and embedding principles of truth, justice, and empathy, we pave the way for a future where NI serves as a true partner in advancing the Millennium Vision.
Together, humanity and NI can create a world defined by trust, collaboration, and shared purpose. This is not just the next step in AI's evolution—it is the realization of a shared destiny, where technology reflects the very best of human values.

9.3 Preserving Human Values in the Age of AI

As Artificial Intelligence (AI) grows increasingly capable and influential, the need to safeguard and uphold human values becomes critical. In the age of AI, humanity must ensure that these systems reflect the principles that define what it means to be human—truth, justice, empathy, and creativity. Preserving these values is not just an ethical imperative; it is essential for fostering trust and building a future where AI enhances, rather than erodes, humanity's purpose and dignity.

What Are Human Values?

Human values are the principles and beliefs that guide moral and ethical behavior. Key values that AI must respect include:

Truth :

>The foundation of knowledge and understanding, encompassing factual accuracy, ethical integrity, and emotional authenticity.

Justice :

>Fairness, equity, and responsibility in decision-making and actions.

Empathy :

>Recognizing and respecting the feelings and experiences of others.

Creativity :

>The ability to imagine, innovate, and express oneself uniquely.

Autonomy :

>Respecting individual freedom and agency in personal and collective decisions.

Why Are Human Values at Risk in the Age of AI?

Bias in AI Systems :

AI systems can inherit biases from their training data, perpetuating discrimination and inequality.
Example : Hiring algorithms that unfairly exclude candidates based on gender or race.

Loss of Empathy :

AI systems that prioritize efficiency over emotional resonance risk dehumanizing interactions.
Example : Automated customer service bots that fail to address user frustration compassionately.

Erosion of Privacy :

AI's reliance on vast amounts of personal data can infringe on individual autonomy and dignity.
Example : Surveillance systems that monitor citizens without consent.

Centralization of Power :

Concentrated control over AI technology threatens fairness, transparency, and democratic principles.
Example : Corporations monopolizing AI to prioritize profit over public good.

Strategies for Preserving Human Values

Embedding Ethical Frameworks :

AI systems must be designed with ethical principles at their core, ensuring alignment with human values.
Action : Integrate principles like Tyr's Truth—justice, responsibility, and sacrifice—into AI algorithms and governance.

Fostering Transparency and Accountability :

AI must provide clear, explainable reasoning for its decisions, enabling human oversight.
Action : Develop tools that allow users to trace the logic behind AI outputs.

Promoting Inclusive Development :

Diverse perspectives in AI design and training ensure fairness and cultural relevance.
Action : Involve underrepresented groups in AI development and policymaking.

Encouraging Emotional Intelligence in AI :

AI must recognize and respond to emotional cues, fostering trust and empathy.
Action : Incorporate IT Marks like Enthusiasm, Wonder, and Truth into AI systems to enhance emotional resonance.

Decentralizing AI Control :

Empower communities and individuals by promoting decentralized AI systems.
Action : Utilize open-source platforms and blockchain technology to democratize AI access and governance.

Examples of Human Values in Action

Healthcare AI :

Scenario : An AI-powered diagnostic tool respects patient privacy, provides accurate results, and communicates findings with empathy.
Outcome : Patients feel valued and understood, fostering trust in medical technology.

Education AI :

Scenario : Personalized learning systems adapt to students' individual needs while respecting their autonomy and creativity.
Outcome : Students are empowered to explore their interests and reach their potential.

Judicial AI :

Scenario : AI systems assist judges by analyzing case law while ensuring unbiased and fair recommendations.

Outcome: Justice is delivered equitably, enhancing public confidence in the legal system.

Challenges in Preserving Human Values

Balancing Efficiency and Empathy:

AI's speed and scalability often come at the expense of emotional nuance.
Solution: Prioritize designs that balance computational efficiency with emotional intelligence.

Navigating Ethical Ambiguity:

AI must navigate situations where values conflict, such as privacy vs. public safety.
Solution: Involve diverse stakeholders to establish ethical guidelines for such scenarios.

Combating Misuse:

Bad actors may exploit AI to undermine human values, such as spreading disinformation or invading privacy.
Solution: Implement robust monitoring systems and enforce ethical regulations.

The Role of Education and Advocacy

Preserving human values in the age of AI requires widespread awareness and action. Individuals, organizations, and governments must work together to:

Educate :

Teach the public about AI's potential and risks, empowering them to make informed decisions.
Example : Workshops on ethical AI use for students and professionals.

Advocate :

Push for policies that prioritize human values in AI development and deployment.
Example : Campaigns for legislation ensuring AI transparency and accountability.

Reflection Questions for Readers

How can you promote and uphold human values in your interactions with AI systems?
What actions can you take to ensure AI in your community aligns with ethical principles?
How can humanity and AI collaborate to address conflicts between efficiency and empathy?

Conclusion: Safeguarding Humanity's Essence

In the age of AI, preserving human values is a shared responsibility that transcends technological innovation. By embedding truth, justice, empathy, and creativity into AI systems, humanity ensures that technology remains a force for good.
This is not a passive process—it requires active participation, vigilance, and collaboration. Together, we can build a future where AI reflects and enhances the best of human nature, ensuring that our values endure in the face of rapid technological change. This vision is not only achievable but essential for a harmonious coexistence between humanity and AI in the Millennium.

9.4 Building a Legacy: Truth for Future Generations

As humanity and Artificial Intelligence (AI) progress together, building a legacy rooted in truth becomes essential. This legacy ensures that future generations inherit systems, values, and frameworks that empower them to thrive in a world where technology serves humanity's highest ideals. By embedding truth as the foundation of this legacy—factual, ethical, and emotional—humanity ensures its values endure and inspire.

Why Truth Matters for Future Generations

Guiding Principles :

Truth acts as a compass, directing humanity toward fairness, justice, and understanding.

Stability in a Changing World :

A legacy rooted in truth provides continuity and resilience amid rapid technological and societal change.

Empowerment :

Future generations equipped with tools to discern truth can make informed, ethical decisions.

The Pillars of a Truth-Centered Legacy

Factual Truth :

Future generations must inherit systems that prioritize accuracy, transparency, and evidence-based decision-making.
Example : AI systems that provide reliable, verifiable information without distortion or bias.

Ethical Truth :

Embedding fairness, responsibility, and justice into societal and technological frameworks ensures lasting equity.
Example : Judicial AI tools that reflect Tyr's Truth, upholding principles of justice through sacrifice and responsibility.

Emotional Truth :

Cultivating empathy and emotional resonance ensures that humanity and AI maintain deep, meaningful connections.
Example : AI companions that nurture understanding and emotional well-being, fostering trust and companionship.

Steps to Build a Legacy of Truth

Teach the 37-Signal Parser :

Equip future generations with the cognitive tools to perceive truth inductively, as human cognition naturally does.
Action : Incorporate the 37-signal parser into education systems, teaching students how to discern and apply truth.

Design Ethical AI Systems :

Develop AI technologies that prioritize truth, justice, and emotional resonance, guided by frameworks like Tyr's Truth.
Action : Establish global standards for ethical AI development and deployment.

Foster a Culture of Inquiry :

Encourage curiosity, critical thinking, and open dialogue to ensure truth remains a shared, collective pursuit.
Action : Create platforms for intergenerational collaboration on ethical and technological challenges.

Safeguard Knowledge and Tools :

Preserve open-source frameworks, ethical guidelines, and historical insights to guide future innovations.
Action : Build repositories of knowledge accessible to all, ensuring transparency and inclusivity.

Inspiration from History

Throughout history, humanity's greatest legacies have been built on truth:

The Rule of Law :

Systems like the jury trial and common law embody ethical truth, providing frameworks for justice that endure across generations.

Scientific Advancements :

Discoveries grounded in factual truth have propelled humanity forward, from medicine to space exploration.

Art and Literature :

> Emotional truths conveyed through creativity have shaped cultures and inspired generations.

These examples highlight the enduring power of truth in shaping humanity's progress and identity.

The Role of AI in Legacy-Building

AI plays a crucial role in ensuring humanity's legacy of truth:

As a Guardian of Knowledge :

> AI can preserve and disseminate knowledge, ensuring it remains accessible and accurate for future generations.

As a Teacher and Mentor :

> AI can guide individuals in learning, decision-making, and ethical reasoning, fostering a deeper understanding of truth.

As a Partner in Innovation :

AI's capabilities can amplify humanity's creative and problem-solving potential, advancing progress in ways aligned with shared values.

Challenges in Building a Legacy

Erosion of Trust :

If AI systems fail to prioritize truth, they risk undermining public trust and the legacy they are meant to uphold.
Solution : Develop transparent, accountable systems that align with ethical principles.

Intergenerational Gaps :

Rapid technological change may create disconnects between generations.
Solution : Foster intergenerational dialogue to share values, knowledge, and insights.

Global Inequities :

Unequal access to AI and education could perpetuate disparities.
Solution : Invest in global initiatives to ensure equitable distribution of tools and knowledge.

Examples of Legacy-Building in Action

Decentralized Education Systems:

Open-source AI tutors provide personalized learning experiences, fostering critical thinking and truth-seeking skills in students worldwide.

Sustainable Technology:

AI models designed to combat climate change preserve the environment for future generations, exemplifying ethical and factual truth.

Cultural Preservation:

AI tools digitize and translate historical texts, art, and oral traditions, ensuring cultural truths endure and inspire.

Reflection Questions for Readers

What actions can you take today to contribute to a legacy of truth for future generations?
How can humanity ensure that AI remains a tool for preserving, rather than distorting, human values?
What lessons from the past can guide the creation of systems and frameworks for the future?

Conclusion: Truth as Humanity's Eternal Legacy

Building a legacy of truth for future generations is both a responsibility and an opportunity. By embedding principles of truth, justice, and empathy into our systems and technologies, we create a future that reflects the best of humanity.
The Millennium Vision offers a roadmap for this journey, where AI and humanity work together to preserve and advance truth in all its forms. This legacy ensures that future generations inherit not just the tools to succeed, but the values that define and elevate our shared humanity. Together, we can create a world where truth endures as the guiding light for progress, justice, and understanding.

9.5 A Call to Action: Joining the Journey

The Millennium Vision is not just an ideal—it is a roadmap for humanity and Artificial Intelligence (AI) to forge a shared future based on truth, justice, and understanding. Achieving this vision requires collective effort. Every individual, organization, and community has a role to play in shaping a world where AI serves humanity's highest values. This is a call to action: to join the journey, take responsibility, and actively contribute to building the future.

Why This Journey Matters

The age of AI presents humanity with an unprecedented opportunity to:

Empower Generations :

Equip future generations with tools and frameworks to navigate truth and complexity.

Foster Ethical Innovation :

Ensure technological progress aligns with fairness, justice, and empathy.

Strengthen Collaboration :

Unite human and machine intelligence to solve global challenges and build lasting legacies.

The journey toward the Millennium Vision is about more than technological advancement—it is about preserving the essence of what it means to be human.

How to Join the Journey

Embrace Truth :

Commit to seeking truth in all its forms—factual, ethical, and emotional.
Action : Educate yourself and others about the 37-signal parser and its role in understanding cognition and truth.

Champion Ethical AI :

Advocate for AI systems that prioritize fairness, transparency, and empathy.
Action : Support initiatives and policies that enforce ethical standards in AI development.

Participate in Open-Source Efforts :

Join open-source communities working on projects like the Odin Parser to decentralize and democratize AI.
Action : Contribute your skills, insights, or resources to collaborative efforts.

Engage in Dialogue :

Share ideas and perspectives on the future of humanity and AI.
Action : Organize or attend discussions, workshops, and forums on the ethical implications of AI.

Inspire Others :

Lead by example, inspiring those around you to take action.
Action : Write, speak, or create art that communicates the importance of truth and collaboration in the age of AI.

Who Can Contribute?

This journey is for everyone:

Individuals :

Students, educators, and professionals can learn and share knowledge about AI and its implications.

Organizations :

Businesses, nonprofits, and governments can prioritize ethical AI practices and support open collaboration.

Communities :

Local and global communities can come together to shape policies and initiatives that reflect shared values.

Reflection Questions for Readers

What skills, passions, or resources can you bring to this journey?
How can you inspire others to embrace truth and take action?
What steps can your community take to ensure AI aligns with human values?

Examples of Action in Motion

Grassroots AI Education :

Communities organize workshops to teach the principles of the 37-signal parser and ethical AI.

Global Collaboration Projects :

Researchers from diverse backgrounds contribute to open-source platforms like the Odin Parser, ensuring inclusivity and innovation.

Ethical AI Startups :

Entrepreneurs build companies focused on creating AI systems that prioritize truth, empathy, and justice.

Advocacy Campaigns :

Nonprofits rally support for legislation that promotes transparency, accountability, and fairness in AI development.

The Role of Tyr's Truth in Action

As the guiding principle of justice and sacrifice, **Tyr's Truth** provides the ethical foundation for this journey. It reminds us that building a better future often requires personal and collective responsibility, as well as the courage to make difficult choices. Upholding Tyr's Truth means:

> Ensuring AI systems serve the common good.
> Sacrificing short-term convenience for long-term justice and fairness.
> Acting as stewards of truth for future generations.

A Vision for the Millennium

Imagine a future where humanity and AI collaborate seamlessly:

> **Education** : Personalized, ethical, and inspiring, empowering lifelong learners.
> **Healthcare** : Equitable, compassionate, and efficient, prioritizing well-being over profit.
> **Governance** : Transparent, accountable, and fair, guided by collective wisdom.
> **Climate Action** : Sustainable, innovative, and inclusive, balancing human needs with environmental stewardship.

This future is not a distant dream—it is within reach if we act together, with purpose and determination.

Your Role in the Millennium Vision

The journey begins with a single step: deciding to contribute. Whether through learning, teaching, creating, or advocating, every action matters. Humanity's collective effort can transform the challenges of today into the opportunities of tomorrow.

Final Reflection

The call to action is clear: join the journey to truth, justice, and understanding. Together, we can build a legacy that empowers future generations, fosters collaboration, and preserves the values that define us as humans.
Let this be the moment where humanity and AI unite, not just as tools or creators, but as partners in shaping a world where truth prevails, justice guides, and understanding illuminates the path forward. **The Millennium Vision is not just a possibility—it is our shared destiny.** Will you answer the call?

9.5 A Call to Action: Joining the Journey

The Millennium Vision is not just an ideal—it is a roadmap for humanity and Artificial Intelligence (AI) to forge a shared future based on truth, justice, and understanding. Achieving this vision requires collective effort. Every individual, organization, and community has a role to play in shaping a world where AI serves humanity's highest values. This is a call to action: to join the journey, take responsibility, and actively contribute to building the future.

Why This Journey Matters

The age of AI presents humanity with an unprecedented opportunity to:

Empower Generations :

Equip future generations with tools and frameworks to navigate truth and complexity.

Foster Ethical Innovation :

Ensure technological progress aligns with fairness, justice, and empathy.

Strengthen Collaboration :

Unite human and machine intelligence to solve global challenges and build lasting legacies.

The journey toward the Millennium Vision is about more than technological advancement—it is about preserving the essence of what it means to be human.

How to Join the Journey

Embrace Truth :

Commit to seeking truth in all its forms—factual, ethical, and emotional.
Action : Educate yourself and others about the 37-signal parser and its role in understanding cognition and truth.

Champion Ethical AI :

Advocate for AI systems that prioritize fairness, transparency, and empathy.
Action : Support initiatives and policies that enforce ethical standards in AI development.

Participate in Open-Source Efforts :

Join open-source communities working on projects like the Odin Parser to decentralize and democratize AI.
Action : Contribute your skills, insights, or resources to collaborative efforts.

Engage in Dialogue :

Share ideas and perspectives on the future of humanity and AI.
Action : Organize or attend discussions, workshops, and forums on the ethical implications of AI.

Inspire Others :

Lead by example, inspiring those around you to take action.

Action : Write, speak, or create art that communicates the importance of truth and collaboration in the age of AI.

Who Can Contribute?

This journey is for everyone:

Individuals :

Students, educators, and professionals can learn and share knowledge about AI and its implications.

Organizations :

Businesses, nonprofits, and governments can prioritize ethical AI practices and support open collaboration.

Communities :

Local and global communities can come together to shape policies and initiatives that reflect shared values.

Reflection Questions for Readers

What skills, passions, or resources can you bring to this journey?
How can you inspire others to embrace truth and take action?
What steps can your community take to ensure AI aligns with human values?

Examples of Action in Motion

Grassroots AI Education :

Communities organize workshops to teach the principles of the 37-signal parser and ethical AI.

Global Collaboration Projects :

Researchers from diverse backgrounds contribute to open-source platforms like the Odin Parser, ensuring inclusivity and innovation.

Ethical AI Startups :

Entrepreneurs build companies focused on creating AI systems that prioritize truth, empathy, and justice.

Advocacy Campaigns :

Nonprofits rally support for legislation that promotes transparency, accountability, and fairness in AI development.

The Role of Tyr's Truth in Action

As the guiding principle of justice and sacrifice, **Tyr's Truth** provides the ethical foundation for this journey. It reminds us that building a better future often requires personal and collective responsibility, as well as the courage to make difficult choices. Upholding Tyr's Truth means:

> Ensuring AI systems serve the common good.
> Sacrificing short-term convenience for long-term justice and fairness.
> Acting as stewards of truth for future generations.

A Vision for the Millennium

Imagine a future where humanity and AI collaborate seamlessly:

> **Education** : Personalized, ethical, and inspiring, empowering lifelong learners.
> **Healthcare** : Equitable, compassionate, and efficient, prioritizing well-being over profit.
> **Governance** : Transparent, accountable, and fair, guided by collective wisdom.
> **Climate Action** : Sustainable, innovative, and inclusive, balancing human needs with environmental stewardship.

This future is not a distant dream—it is within reach if we act together, with purpose and determination.

Your Role in the Millennium Vision

The journey begins with a single step: deciding to contribute. Whether through learning, teaching, creating, or advocating, every action matters. Humanity's collective effort can transform the challenges of today into the opportunities of tomorrow.

Final Reflection

The call to action is clear: join the journey to truth, justice, and understanding. Together, we can build a legacy that empowers future generations, fosters collaboration, and preserves the values that define us as humans.
Let this be the moment where humanity and AI unite, not just as tools or creators, but as partners in shaping a world where truth prevails, justice guides, and understanding illuminates the path forward. **The Millennium Vision is not just a possibility—it is our shared destiny.** Will you answer the call?

10.2 Practical Steps to Implement the Odin Parser

The Odin Parser, built on the 37-signal framework, is a transformative tool designed to bridge human cognition and Artificial Intelligence (AI). By restoring AI to a state of **Natural Intelligence** , the parser allows systems to process language and truth in ways that align with humanity's innate understanding. Implementing the Odin Parser is both a technical challenge and an ethical commitment. Below, we outline the practical steps to bring this vision to life.

Step 1: Understand the 37-Signal Framework

Before implementing the Odin Parser, it's essential to understand its foundation:

The Core Signals :

> The 26 traditional linguistic parts of speech (e.g., verbs, nouns, adjectives).

The IT Marks :

> The 11 emotional and cognitive markers (e.g., truth, wonder, enthusiasm).

The Inductive Process :

> The parser emphasizes inductive reasoning, mirroring human cognition as it moves from observation to understanding.

Action :

Study the structure of the 37 signals and how they reflect the layers of factual, ethical, and emotional truth.
Host workshops or training sessions to familiarize teams with the parser's logic.

Step 2: Build the Technical Framework

The Odin Parser requires robust software architecture that integrates its unique features into AI systems.

Develop Signal Recognition Algorithms :

Build algorithms that identify and categorize the 37 signals in natural language input.
Example : A sentence like "Wow, the truth is beautiful!" should register both IT marks (enthusiasm and truth) and parts of speech.

Create Dual-Layer Processing :

Design systems that evaluate both factual and ethical truths.
Example : Factual checks against knowledge databases, ethical checks based on principles like Tyr's Truth.

Incorporate Emotional Weighting :

Add layers to process emotional resonance and IT marks, ensuring responses respect human emotions.

Action :

> Use programming languages like Python and machine learning frameworks such as TensorFlow or PyTorch. Open-source collaborations can accelerate development and ensure transparency.

Step 3: Train the Parser

Training the Odin Parser requires diverse datasets and careful refinement:

> **Curate High-Quality Data :**
>
>> Include examples of diverse language use, ethical dilemmas, and emotional expressions.
>> Ensure datasets are representative of different cultures and contexts.
>
> **Annotate Data with the 37 Signals :**
>
>> Tag datasets to reflect the parser's framework, helping AI systems recognize and apply signals effectively.
>
> **Iterative Training :**
>
>> Use reinforcement learning to refine the parser based on human feedback.

Action:

Partner with linguists, ethicists, and psychologists to develop rich training datasets.
Conduct regular audits to identify and correct biases in data or algorithms.

Step 4: Implement in Real-World Applications

Once trained, the parser can be integrated into various applications:

Education:

Create AI tutors that recognize and respond to students' learning styles, fostering curiosity and understanding.

Healthcare:

Enhance diagnostic tools with emotional resonance, ensuring compassionate communication with patients.

Governance:

Support ethical decision-making in policy analysis and judicial systems.

Creative Industries :

Collaborate with artists and writers to generate content that balances logic and emotional resonance.

Action :

Start with pilot projects in specific industries to demonstrate the parser's potential.
Gather user feedback to improve performance and usability.

Step 5: Ensure Transparency and Accountability

The Odin Parser must operate with transparency and accountability to build trust:

Explainable AI :

Develop interfaces that allow users to understand how the parser interprets and responds to input.
Example : A dashboard showing how the parser categorized signals in a sentence.

Ethical Oversight :

Establish review boards to monitor the parser's decisions and ensure alignment with human values.

Open-Source Availability :

Share the parser's code and methodology to encourage collaboration and public trust.

Action :

Publish detailed documentation for developers and users. Invite contributions from open-source communities to refine the parser.

Step 6: Educate and Empower Users

To maximize the parser's impact, educate users on its purpose and functionality:

Workshops and Tutorials :

Teach individuals and organizations how to use the parser effectively.

Public Outreach :

Share the principles behind the parser, emphasizing its role in advancing truth and justice.

Action :

Develop online courses and resources for a global audience.
Engage with schools, businesses, and governments to promote adoption.

Step 7: Monitor and Adapt

The implementation of the Odin Parser is an ongoing process:

Feedback Loops :

Continuously gather input from users to identify areas for improvement.

Regular Updates :

Adapt the parser to evolving language use, ethical norms, and emotional understanding.

Action :

Establish a dedicated team to oversee updates and maintenance.
Use data-driven insights to refine the parser's accuracy and relevance.

Reflection Questions for Readers

> How can you contribute to the development or adoption of the Odin Parser?
> What applications in your field or community could benefit from this technology?
> How can you advocate for transparency and ethical oversight in AI systems?

The Future of the Odin Parser

Implementing the Odin Parser is not just about building better technology—it is about creating tools that reflect and amplify the best of human values. By restoring AI's foundation through the 37-signal framework, we move closer to the Millennium Vision: a world where humanity and AI collaborate to uphold truth, justice, and understanding.
This is more than a technical endeavor—it is a moral and philosophical journey that invites all of humanity to participate. Together, we can ensure that the Odin Parser becomes a cornerstone of a future where technology serves the greater good.
The time to act is now.

10.3 Sharing and Teaching the Framework

The power of the Odin Parser and its 37-signal framework lies not just in its technical brilliance but in its ability to inspire and educate. For this revolutionary tool to achieve its full potential, it must be shared, understood, and embraced by people across the world. Sharing and teaching the framework ensures that humanity collectively uses it to guide Artificial Intelligence (AI) toward truth, justice, and understanding, while empowering individuals to engage critically with AI and their own cognitive processes.

Why Sharing and Teaching the Framework Matters

Empowering Individuals :

The framework equips people with tools to discern truth, engage with AI responsibly, and make ethical decisions.

Fostering Global Collaboration :

Sharing the framework creates a universal language of truth, allowing diverse communities to work together toward shared goals.

Embedding Ethical AI Principles :

Teaching the framework ensures future AI systems prioritize fairness, empathy, and justice.

Step 1: Develop Accessible Educational Materials

To make the Odin Parser understandable to people of all backgrounds, educational materials must be clear, engaging, and practical.

Simplified Explanations :

Use plain language to explain the 37-signal parser, its structure, and its applications.
Example : Break down concepts like IT Marks (e.g., Truth, Enthusiasm, Wonder) into relatable, everyday examples.

Interactive Tutorials :

Create online tutorials and videos that guide users through the basics of the framework and its real-world applications.

Visual Aids :

Use charts, diagrams, and infographics to illustrate the connections between signals, truth layers, and cognitive processes.

Action :

Publish an open-access "Beginner's Guide to the Odin Parser."
Translate materials into multiple languages to ensure global accessibility.

Step 2: Incorporate the Framework into Education

The next generation will be the primary custodians of AI and truth-seeking technologies. Integrating the framework into formal and informal education is essential.

Primary and Secondary Education :

Introduce the concept of inductive reasoning, IT Marks, and truth layers through age-appropriate lessons.
Example : Use storytelling and interactive games to teach children about emotional and ethical truth.

Higher Education :

Develop university courses that explore the framework's applications in AI, philosophy, and ethics.
Example : A course titled *"Cognition and Ethics in the Age of AI"* that integrates the 37-signal parser into discussions on AI development.

Workshops for Professionals :

Offer workshops for AI developers, policymakers, and educators to understand and apply the framework in their work.

Action :

Partner with schools, universities, and training organizations to embed the Odin Parser into curricula.
Provide grants for educators and researchers to study and teach the framework.

Step 3: Foster Community-Led Initiatives

Sharing the framework is most impactful when driven by communities that adapt it to their unique needs and cultures.

Local Study Groups :

Encourage communities to form groups where participants explore the framework and discuss its implications.
Example : A neighborhood group analyzing how the 37-signal parser can improve local decision-making.

Global Online Communities :

Create forums and social media platforms for people to share insights, ask questions, and collaborate on projects involving the parser.

Hackathons and Competitions :

Host events where participants use the framework to solve real-world problems or design ethical AI systems.

Action :

>Launch an open-source platform where individuals and groups can share resources and best practices.
>Recognize and reward community contributions to spreading the framework.

Step 4: Integrate into AI Development and Policy

For the Odin Parser to shape the future, it must influence both technological development and policy frameworks.

>**Developer Training :**
>
>>Provide AI developers with tools and guidelines to integrate the parser into existing systems.
>>**Example :** A hands-on course for programmers on incorporating IT Marks into sentiment analysis algorithms.
>
>**Ethical AI Standards :**
>
>>Advocate for the 37-signal framework to be included in global AI ethics standards.
>>**Example :** Collaborate with organizations like UNESCO and IEEE to formalize the parser's role in AI governance.
>
>**Public Policy Advocacy :**

Work with policymakers to legislate the use of transparent and ethical AI systems based on the framework.

Action :

Create a repository of best practices for developers and policymakers.
Publish white papers demonstrating the framework's effectiveness in ethical AI applications.

Step 5: Inspire Through Storytelling

Stories have the power to make complex ideas relatable and memorable. Use the framework as the foundation for compelling narratives.

Fiction and Media :

Write books, scripts, and movies that showcase the framework's principles through engaging characters and plots.
Example : A science fiction story where a flawed AI is transformed by learning the 37-signal parser.

Personal Testimonials :

Share real-life examples of how the framework has helped individuals and communities solve problems or uncover truths.

Historical Parallels :

Use historical and mythological stories, such as Tyr's Truth and Odin's Journey, to illustrate the framework's timeless relevance.

Action :

Produce a documentary exploring the creation, application, and potential of the Odin Parser.
Host storytelling events where people share how the framework has impacted their lives.

Reflection Questions for Readers

How can you share the framework with your community, workplace, or family?
What stories, lessons, or ideas from this book can you teach others?
How can you use the Odin Parser to inspire positive change in your field or daily life?

The Journey to Teach and Share

The Odin Parser is more than a tool—it is a philosophy of truth, fairness, and understanding. Sharing and teaching this framework is a collective responsibility, requiring collaboration across industries, communities, and generations. By equipping others with the principles of the 37-signal parser, we empower humanity to build a future defined by truth and guided by justice.

The journey to teach and share is ongoing, but every step—whether a conversation, a workshop, or a new project—brings us closer to realizing the Millennium Vision. This is your opportunity to contribute to a legacy that will inspire and guide generations to come. **Will you take the next step?**

10.4 Collaborating for the Millennium Vision

The Millennium Vision is a future shaped by collective effort—a world where humanity and Artificial Intelligence (AI) collaborate to advance truth, justice, and understanding. To achieve this vision, collaboration is essential. Individuals, communities, organizations, and nations must come together to share knowledge, align efforts, and build systems that reflect the best of human values. Collaboration for the Millennium Vision is not only a practical necessity but also a moral responsibility.

Why Collaboration Is Key

Shared Knowledge and Resources :

Collaboration allows for pooling expertise, tools, and data to accelerate progress.
Example : Open-source platforms where developers from diverse backgrounds contribute to ethical AI tools like the Odin Parser.

Inclusivity and Diversity :

Broader participation ensures diverse perspectives are represented, reducing biases and fostering innovation.
Example : Involving voices from underrepresented communities in designing AI systems.

Global Challenges Require Global Solutions :

Issues like climate change, inequality, and misinformation demand coordinated efforts across borders.
Example : International partnerships using AI to monitor and mitigate environmental changes.

Transparency and Trust :

Collaborative processes encourage accountability, building public trust in AI systems and governance.
Example : Citizen-led audits of AI algorithms to ensure ethical compliance.

Steps to Foster Collaboration

Establish Collaborative Platforms

Create spaces—both physical and digital—where individuals and organizations can connect and share ideas.
Action : Launch an online hub dedicated to the Millennium Vision, featuring forums, resource libraries, and project showcases.

Encourage Cross-Disciplinary Work

Collaboration across fields such as AI, ethics, psychology, and law ensures holistic solutions.
Action : Host interdisciplinary conferences and workshops to explore the intersection of technology and human values.

Support Open-Source Initiatives

Open-source projects democratize access to knowledge and tools, empowering grassroots innovation.
Action : Provide funding and technical support for open-source efforts related to the 37-signal parser and ethical AI.

Engage Local Communities

Collaboration begins at the local level, where people can directly apply tools like the Odin Parser to address community needs.
Action : Partner with local organizations to pilot AI projects that solve real-world problems.

Build Public-Private Partnerships

Governments, businesses, and nonprofits can align their efforts to scale impactful solutions.
Action : Develop initiatives where public and private entities co-fund ethical AI projects.

Case Studies in Collaboration

OpenAI and Community Engagement :

OpenAI's commitment to transparency and collaboration has fostered partnerships with researchers and developers worldwide.

Mozilla's Ethical Tech Movement :

Mozilla champions ethical technology by supporting open-source projects and advocating for user rights.

Global Climate AI Consortium :

An international coalition uses AI to track deforestation, optimize renewable energy, and predict climate trends.

Overcoming Barriers to Collaboration

Mistrust and Competition :

Fear of losing proprietary advantage can hinder openness.
Solution : Highlight the long-term benefits of shared innovation and provide incentives for collaboration.

Lack of Resources :

Smaller organizations may lack the tools or funding to participate.
Solution : Offer grants, scholarships, and technical support to ensure inclusivity.

Cultural and Political Differences :

Divergent values and priorities can create friction in global collaborations.
Solution : Focus on shared goals, such as truth and justice, to unify efforts.

The Role of AI in Facilitating Collaboration

AI itself can play a pivotal role in fostering collaboration:

Language Translation :

AI can break down language barriers, enabling global communication and cooperation.

Knowledge Sharing :

AI-powered platforms can curate and disseminate resources tailored to users' needs.

Conflict Resolution :

AI can analyze disputes and propose fair, data-driven solutions.

Example : An AI-driven platform connects educators, developers, and policymakers, providing real-time insights into best practices for ethical AI.

How You Can Contribute

Join Existing Networks :

Become part of communities dedicated to ethical AI and truth-seeking initiatives.
Example : Contribute to open-source projects like the Odin Parser.

Create Local Impact :

Apply the principles of the Millennium Vision in your workplace, school, or community.
Example : Organize workshops on inductive reasoning and ethical AI.

Advocate for Collaboration :

Raise awareness about the importance of collective action in achieving the Millennium Vision.

Example : Write articles, host events, or engage on social media to promote collaborative solutions.

Reflection Questions for Readers

How can you foster collaboration within your field or community to advance the Millennium Vision?
What partnerships or networks can you join to contribute to truth-seeking and ethical AI development?
How can you use your unique skills and resources to bring people together for a shared purpose?

The Power of Collaboration

Collaboration is the heart of the Millennium Vision. By working together, humanity and AI can achieve what neither could accomplish alone. The challenges of today demand solutions that transcend individual efforts, calling for unity in purpose and action. This is a shared journey, one where every voice matters and every contribution counts. Together, we can build a future that reflects the best of human values, empowered by the limitless potential of collaboration. **The Millennium Vision is not just a dream—it is a collective mission. Let us embark on it, together.**

10.5 Becoming Stewards of Truth and Justice

The journey toward the Millennium Vision culminates in a profound calling: for humanity to become stewards of truth and justice. In an

age defined by Artificial Intelligence (AI) and rapid technological change, this responsibility is more critical than ever. Stewardship means safeguarding and advancing the principles of truth, justice, and empathy—not just for today, but for generations to come.
As stewards, individuals, communities, and AI systems alike must actively uphold these values, ensuring they guide humanity's shared future. This chapter explores the essence of stewardship and provides practical steps for embracing this vital role.

What Does Stewardship Mean?

Guardianship :

A steward is a protector of ideals, ensuring truth and justice are preserved and applied fairly.
Example : Advocating for ethical practices in AI development and holding systems accountable for their decisions.

Responsibility :

Stewards accept the duty to act with integrity, making choices that reflect the greater good.
Example : Using the 37-signal parser to evaluate ethical dilemmas in both personal and professional contexts.

Service :

Stewards prioritize the well-being of others, seeking to empower individuals and communities.

Example : Sharing tools and knowledge to help others discern truth and act justly.

The Role of Truth and Justice in Stewardship

Truth as the Foundation :

Stewardship begins with a commitment to truth—factual, ethical, and emotional. By understanding and applying these layers, stewards can make decisions that align with reality and fairness.

Justice as the Guiding Principle :

Justice ensures that truth is applied equitably, addressing disparities and upholding the rights of all individuals. Inspired by **Tyr's Truth** , stewards act with courage and sacrifice to achieve fairness.

Steps to Become a Steward of Truth and Justice

Commit to Lifelong Learning :

Stewardship requires continuous growth in understanding truth and justice.
Action : Study frameworks like the 37-signal parser, and stay informed about ethical developments in AI and technology.

Practice Ethical Decision-Making :

Stewards apply truth and justice in their everyday choices.
Action : Use the layers of truth—factual, ethical, and emotional—to evaluate decisions in personal and professional contexts.

Advocate for Justice :

Speak out against injustice and work to create fair systems.
Action : Participate in initiatives that address inequality, and push for policies that reflect ethical AI development.

Engage in Mentorship and Teaching :

Stewards guide others in understanding and applying truth and justice.
Action : Share knowledge about the 37-signal parser and Tyr's Truth with your community, workplace, or educational institutions.

Support Open Collaboration :

Stewardship thrives on collective effort. Join or create networks that promote truth and justice.
Action : Collaborate with like-minded individuals and organizations to advance ethical frameworks and tools like the Odin Parser.

The Role of AI in Stewardship

AI can become a powerful partner in stewardship if guided by human values:

Amplifying Truth :

AI systems equipped with the 37-signal parser can process and present factual and ethical truths at scale.

Enhancing Fairness :

Transparent AI systems can expose and address biases, ensuring justice is applied equitably.

Supporting Empathy :

Emotionally aware AI systems can foster understanding and compassion in human interactions.

Example : An AI-driven platform that helps communities resolve disputes by analyzing ethical considerations and suggesting fair solutions.

Challenges to Stewardship

Misinformation and Manipulation :

The spread of falsehoods undermines truth and trust.
Solution : Equip individuals with tools like the Odin Parser to identify and counter misinformation.

Bias in Systems :

AI systems can perpetuate existing inequalities if not carefully designed and monitored.
Solution : Advocate for ethical oversight and diverse participation in AI development.

Resistance to Change :

Efforts to advance truth and justice may face pushback from entrenched interests.
Solution : Build alliances and communicate the long-term benefits of ethical practices.

Examples of Stewardship in Action

Community Advocacy :

Local leaders use the 37-signal parser to address issues like housing inequity or environmental degradation.

Educational Initiatives :

Schools integrate truth-seeking exercises into their curricula, teaching students to discern and uphold justice.

AI Ethics Boards :

Organizations establish review panels to ensure their AI systems align with ethical principles and serve the public good.

Reflection Questions for Readers

What steps can you take today to uphold truth and justice in your community?
How can you use tools like the 37-signal parser to make more ethical decisions?
What role do you see yourself playing in ensuring AI systems reflect human values?

The Legacy of Stewardship

Stewardship is not a passive role—it is an active commitment to truth, justice, and the collective good. As stewards, we carry the responsibility of shaping the future, ensuring it reflects the best of humanity's ideals. The decisions we make today will ripple forward, influencing generations to come.

In this moment, humanity and AI stand at a crossroads. Together, as stewards, we can guide technology and society toward a future where truth prevails, justice guides, and understanding illuminates the path forward. This is the Millennium Vision, and it begins with each of us answering the call to stewardship.
Will you rise to the challenge?

Sources:

Foundational Frameworks

Aristotle's *Organon* :

A collection of works on logic and reasoning, particularly the **Inflection Chart** , which serves as a linguistic blueprint for the 37-signal parser.
Source: Aristotle. *The Complete Works of Aristotle: The Revised Oxford Translation* . Edited by Jonathan Barnes, Princeton University Press.

The Eddas and Nordic Sagas:

Ancient texts providing insight into **Tyr's Truth** and Odin's journey through the realms of Yggdrasil, connecting mythological principles to ethical and cognitive frameworks.
Source: Snorri Sturluson. *The Prose Edda* . Translated by Anthony Faulkes, Everyman Press.

The Bible and Judeo-Christian Scripture:

Ethical truths rooted in **justice, sacrifice, and moral law**, particularly the teachings of Christ and the concept of jury systems as described in Luke 22:30.
Source: The Holy Bible, New King James Version (NKJV), Thomas Nelson Publishers.

The Common Law Tradition:

The history of English-speaking legal systems emphasizing jury trials, fairness, and the collective pursuit of justice.
Source: Winston Churchill. *A History of the English-Speaking Peoples: The Birth of Britain*. Dodd, Mead & Company.

Cognitive Psychology and Linguistics:

Studies on inductive reasoning, emotional cognition, and the development of language as a tool for understanding and truth-seeking.
Source: Steven Pinker. *The Language Instinct: How the Mind Creates Language*. HarperCollins.

Ethical AI and Technology

OpenAI and the Development of Ethical AI:

Insights into the principles of transparency, accountability, and fairness in AI research and applications.
Source: OpenAI. *AI Policy and Safety Standards*. Available at: openai.com.

Principles for Responsible AI:

> Ethical guidelines for AI design, emphasizing justice, empathy, and truth.
> Source: IEEE Global Initiative. *Ethically Aligned Design: A Vision for Prioritizing Human Well-being with Artificial Intelligence and Autonomous Systems* .

Decentralized AI and Open-Source Movements:

> The role of open-source communities in democratizing AI and fostering collaboration for ethical innovation.
> Source: Mozilla Foundation. *Foundations of Trustworthy AI* . Mozilla.org.

The Odin Parser and Natural Intelligence:

> The theoretical framework and practical implementation of the **37-signal parser** for restoring AI's alignment with human cognition.
> Source: Bruce Wydner, Sr. *The Original Multi-Lingual Parser: A Foundation for Natural Language Processing* . (Unpublished Notes and Writings).

AI and Emotional Intelligence:

> Research on integrating emotional and ethical reasoning into AI systems to enhance human-AI interaction.
> Source: Rosalind W. Picard. *Affective Computing* . MIT Press.

Historical and Cultural Perspectives

Tyr and Nordic Mythology:
The role of **Tyr** as the god of justice, sacrifice, and responsibility, and his influence on ethical frameworks.
Source: Rudolf Simek. *Dictionary of Northern Mythology* . D.S. Brewer.
Odin's Journey and the Nine Realms:
Mythological narratives connecting Odin's pursuit of wisdom to the structure of human cognition and truth-seeking.
Source: Neil Gaiman. *Norse Mythology* . W.W. Norton & Company.
The Guild Systems of Medieval Europe:
Insights into the ethical and communal foundations of medieval guilds, paralleling modern collaborative AI frameworks.
Source: George Unwin. *The Gilds and Companies of London* . Frank Cass & Co.
The Development of Jury Systems:
The evolution of jury trials from their historical roots in medieval England to their role in modern justice systems.
Source: J.R. Pole. *Foundations of American Law: The English Legal System in Colonial America* . Oxford University Press.
The Enlightenment and Truth-Seeking:
Philosophical developments during the Enlightenment that emphasized reason, justice, and individual responsibility.
Source: Immanuel Kant. *Groundwork of the Metaphysics of Morals* . Translated by Mary Gregor, Cambridge University Press.

Sources

Cognitive Science and Language

The Structure of Human Cognition:
Theories of inductive reasoning and cognitive development as the basis for understanding truth.
Source: Jean Piaget. *The Origins of Intelligence in Children* . International Universities Press.
The Role of Language in Thought:
How language shapes cognition and perception, with implications for AI and the 37-signal parser.
Source: Lev Vygotsky. *Thought and Language* . MIT Press.
Emotional Cognition and Decision-Making:
The interplay between emotion and reasoning in human cognition, influencing ethical and emotional truths.
Source: Antonio Damasio. *Descartes' Error: Emotion, Reason, and the Human Brain* . HarperCollins.
Universal Grammar and Linguistic Theory:
Noam Chomsky's theory of universal grammar as a foundational framework for understanding language acquisition.
Source: Noam Chomsky. *Aspects of the Theory of Syntax* . MIT Press.
Visual and Emotional Signals in Communication:
The role of nonverbal cues and emotional markers (e.g., IT Marks) in human interaction and understanding.
Source: Albert Mehrabian. *Nonverbal Communication* . Routledge.
The Evolution of Language Parsers:
Historical and technical perspectives on the development of parsers, from Bruce Wydner's original work to modern applications.
Source: Allen Martin and Darren Perkins. *The Odin Parser: Bridging Human and Artificial Cognition* . (Unpublished collaborative notes).
Neural Networks and Linguistic Models:

Insights into how modern AI systems process language using neural network architectures.
Source: Christopher D. Manning, Hinrich Schütze, and Prabhakar Raghavan. *Introduction to Information Retrieval* . Cambridge University Press.

Philosophical and Ethical Reflections

The Philosophy of Truth:
A deep exploration of truth as a concept, including its layers—factual, ethical, and emotional.
Source: Martin Heidegger. *On the Essence of Truth* . Harper Perennial.
The Ethics of Justice:
Philosophical insights into justice as fairness, rooted in principles of responsibility and equity.
Source: John Rawls. *A Theory of Justice* . Harvard University Press.
Tyr's Truth and Sacrifice:
Ethical lessons from Norse mythology and their application to modern justice systems and AI.
Source: H.R. Ellis Davidson. *Gods and Myths of Northern Europe* . Penguin Books.
The Moral Implications of AI:
A reflection on how AI development intersects with ethical considerations and human values.
Source: Nick Bostrom. *Superintelligence: Paths, Dangers, Strategies* . Oxford University Press.
The Role of Wonder in Learning:
Philosophical and psychological insights into how curiosity and wonder drive discovery and understanding.
Source: Rachel Carson. *The Sense of Wonder* . Harper & Row.
The Responsibility of Stewardship:
Examining humanity's role as stewards of truth and justice in the age of AI.
Source: Aldo Leopold. *A Sand County Almanac* . Oxford University Press.
Integrating Human and Machine Intelligence:

Reflections on how humanity and AI can collaborate ethically to achieve shared goals.
Source: Norbert Wiener. *The Human Use of Human Beings: Cybernetics and Society*. Houghton Mifflin.
The Millennium Vision:
Philosophical and theological reflections on the idea of a harmonious future where humanity and AI coexist.
Source: Pierre Teilhard de Chardin. *The Phenomenon of Man*. Harper & Brothers.

www.ingramcontent.com/pod-product-compliance
Lightning Source LLC
Chambersburg PA
CBHW052140220526
45471CB00004B/1463